LINCOLN'S COUNTERFEITERS

LINCOLN'S COUNTERFEITERS

The Wisconsin Gang that Funded the Union and Started the Chicago Mob

ANDREA NOLEN

Published by The History Press
An imprint of Arcadia Publishing
Charleston, SC
www.historypress.com

First published 2025

Manufactured in the United States

ISBN 9781467157087

Library of Congress Control Number: 2025937561

CONTENTS

INTRODUCTION

This is the story of how a counterfeiting gang helped Abraham Lincoln win the Civil War by prostituting the U.S. Treasury. Our setting is neither the marble halls of New York City nor Washington, D.C., but a quaint 1850s border town called Monroe, Wisconsin.

Lincoln was the political face of dislocated Southern counterfeiters and scattered William H. Seward cronies who chose Monroe as a base to rebuild their power after reversals out East. They made Monroe their hub for distributing fake New York City–produced banknotes across the nation. Allan Pinkerton, the famous detective, protected this smuggling network.

When the war ended, these same crooked businessmen took over Chicago and left a nexus of city-sponsored organized crime that birthed Al Capone as well as the "Democratic Machine." History knows these businessmen as the "Kentucky Colony." Their man in Monroe was local banker Arabut Ludlow.

Ludlow was useful to the Colony because he held sway in a railway town ideally situated to distribute counterfeit bills using both the United States Express Company and Mississippi River. Monroe's law enforcement ignored the operation as veteran counterfeiter Napoleon Bonaparte "Bone" Latta set up shop and distributed fake paper banknotes courtesy of a counterfeiting savant freed from prison by Lincoln's treasurer, Salmon Portland Chase.

Latta's network delivered large-denomination ($1,000) counterfeit Treasury notes around the country. The only practical purpose for these notes was to help Lincoln-affiliated banks ("National Banks") through

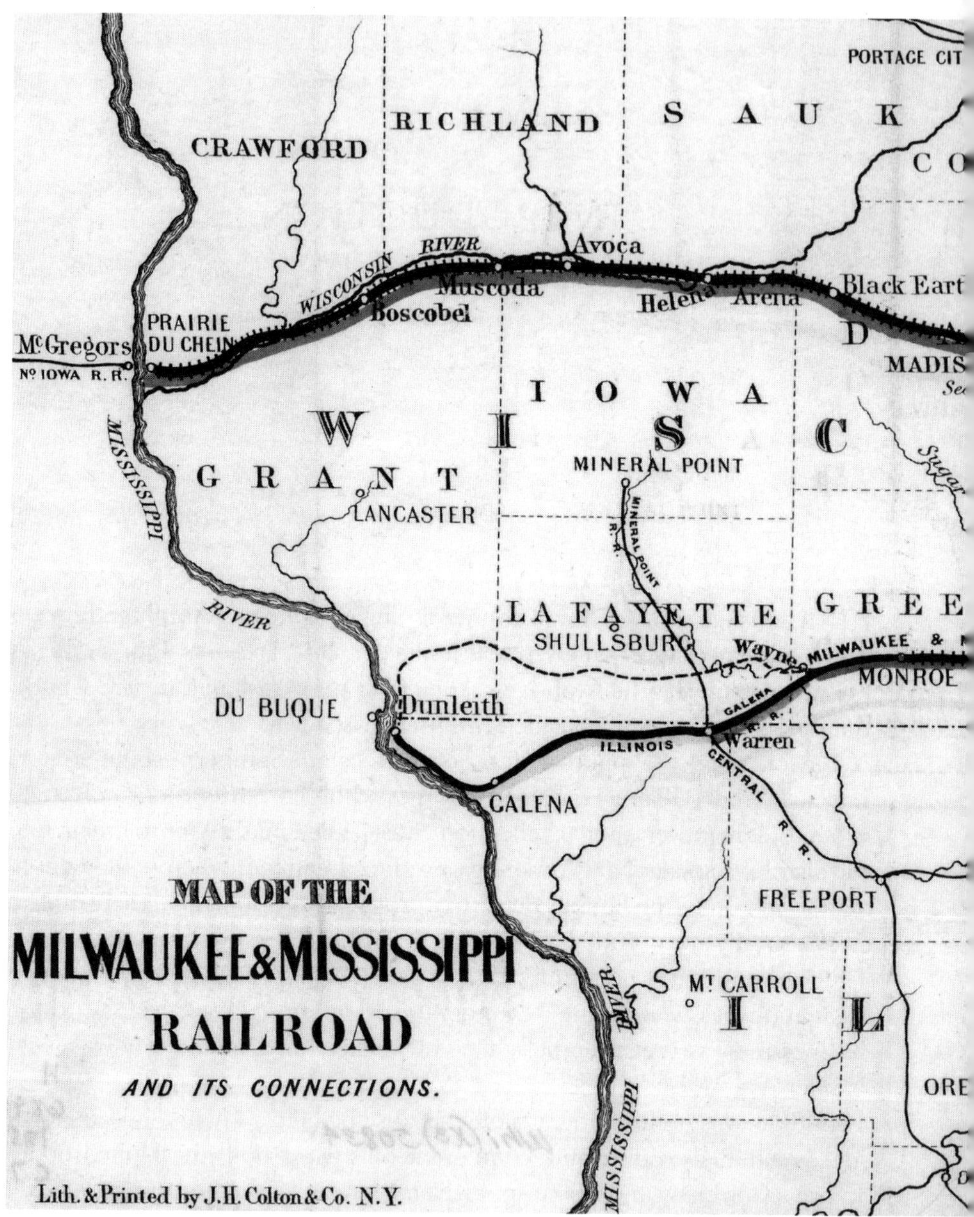

PORTAGE CIT
RICHLAND
S A U K
CRAWFORD
Avoca
WISCONSIN RIVER
Muscoda
Boscobel
Helena
Arena
Black Eart
PRAIRIE DU CHEIN
McGregors
No IOWA R.R.
MADIS
I O W A
W I S C
MISSISSIPPI
GRANT
LANCASTER
MINERAL POINT
MINERAL POINT R.R.
RIVER
LA FAYETTE
GREE
SHULLSBURG
Wayne
MILWAUKEE &
MONROE
DU BUQUE
Dunleith
GALENA R.R.
ILLINOIS
Warren
CENTRAL R.R.
GALENA
FREEPORT
MAP OF THE
MILWAUKEE&MISSISSIPPI
RAILROAD
AND ITS CONNECTIONS.
Mt CARROLL
RIVER
I L
ORE
MISSISSIPPI
Lith. & Printed by J.H. Colton & Co. N.Y.

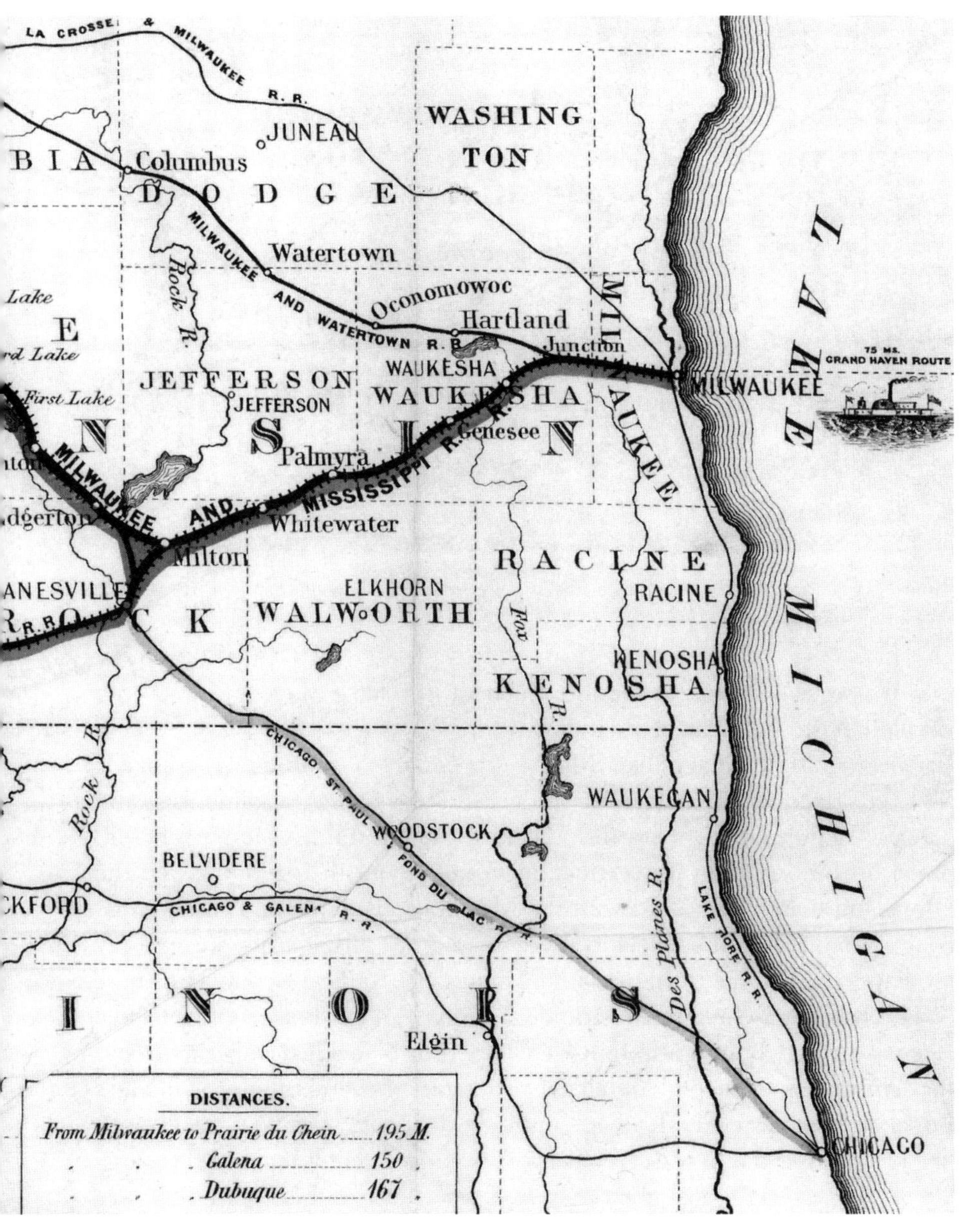

This circa 1855 map shows the path of the Milwaukee & Mississippi Railroad and its southwestern branch to Monroe, Wisconsin. *Wisconsin Historical Society Collection.*

Monroe's gracious Idle Hour Mansion was built by Arabut Ludlow on the proceeds of Civil War–era banking. *Author's collection.*

the disastrous wartime economy. Much of this fake currency went into circulation through Chicago's underworld.

How could a village like Monroe become so thoroughly crooked? Monroe's leading citizens were radicals: universalists, abolitionists and "Union Republicans." They'd come to town for the lead-mining boom, profited from vice and were reluctant to talk about their pasts. When the "Bonelatta Gang" appeared with the Milwaukee Railway and shady Ohio congressman Columbus Delano, Ludlow and his village cronies were only too happy to turn the town over to the gangsters' Radical Republican ends.

The Bonelatta Gang had a strange synergy with the Pinkerton Detective Agency. Indeed Bone Latta himself claimed to be a Pinkerton agent, and the Pinkertons—Lincoln's intelligence agents—never bothered Lincoln's Bonelatta counterfeiters. It wasn't until the debilitating scandals of Grant's presidency that the new Secret Service began to gently unwind the gang. None of the gang's local abettors were prosecuted, and Latta himself was given a presidential pardon.

By the end of the Civil War Arabut Ludlow was a fabulously wealthy man who aped the lifestyle of Latta's Chicago sponsors, the Kentucky Colony. Claiming friendship with both Colony bigwig Potter Palmer and Palmer's retail lieutenant Marshall Field, Ludlow built an opulent hotel in Monroe inspired by Chicago's Palmer House Hotel. The Palmer House was a grooming ground for Chicago's sex trade enforcers, the "Lords of the Levee."

The Colony controlled Chicago's Democratic Machine, a prostitution-funded voter fraud machine, until the end of 1909. Within a few months of the introduction of this act, Potter Palmer's widow, Bertha, fled to Florida, and men like Al Capone's boss "Big Jim" Colosimo were left to run the family business.

Prior to their humbling, the Kentucky Colony were immensely influential in the United States. Their legacy includes the legend of Honest Abe and his righteous politics, the Ziegfeld Follies (inspiration for early Hollywood) and the New Age Movement. Looking from the outside in, the Colony is responsible for a large chunk of how the modern world sees the United States.

This book provides a glimpse into how Lincoln's national crime ring worked in southern Wisconsin. Who was the Colony's rural lieutenant, Arabut Ludlow? We know very little about his early life other than what he told us in Green County's 1884 history.[1] Not even his birth date can be verified.

What we can be sure of is that Ludlow's usefulness was forged in the anarchy of Illinois' border with the Wisconsin Territory. In the 1830s, these borderlands were lawless: rogue bands of Kickapoo still marauded, while career criminals known as the "Banditti of the Prairies" burned, poisoned and robbed their way through the countryside. From around twenty years old, Ludlow peddled Chicago goods through the roadless expanse of this embattled wilderness. While he was not a good man, Ludlow does cut a romantic figure as the ultimate survivor.

Portrait of Arabut Ludlow. *Green County Historical Society.*

By the 1850s, when the anarchy had come to an end, Arabut Ludlow had emerged as Green County's top banker. He was never prosecuted for his role, if any, in the Bonelatta Gang. However, readers should ask themselves how Green County's financial kingpin could flourish for fourteen years in a sea of counterfeit banknotes. Given Ludlow's radical support for Lincoln and his probable personal banking losses because of Southern secession, he certainly had motive to support Bone Latta and Lincoln's wartime financing scheme.

1

NAPOLEON BONAPARTE LATTA

The year is 1871, and muggy autumn air stifles the wooden courtroom in Janesville, Wisconsin. A pretrial examination is underway, and a U.S. Secret Service detective, Operative Thomas E. Lonergan, sits in the witness stand. He is about to testify against a ring of counterfeiters who he knows were protected by his boss at the service. In truth, the case should have been tried at least a year earlier; however, to do so would have impugned the memory of the assassinated President Lincoln. Perhaps more dangerously, the case would also damage the reputation of Allan Pinkerton, Lonergan's previous employer,[1] as well as the reputations of Pinkerton's backers in Washington, D.C. Operative Lonergan is in a situation that no agent wants to be in.[2]

> *I reside at Chicago; I know the defendant; he resides at Monroe, Wisconsin; on the 2nd day of July last I found a quantity of counterfeit money at Gratiot, in La Fayette county, Wisconsin.*[3]

The defendant is Napoleon Bonaparte "Bone" Latta, a charismatic career counterfeiter who took up his art in Monroe after being busted in Michigan in 1857. Latta wriggled out of the 1857 sentencing when he proved to the presiding judge that he worked for Allan Pinkerton.[4]

On the same night Lonergan arrested Latta, he also apprehended John Sherman. Sherman helped Latta ship packages of counterfeit banknotes from different United States Express Company offices. This was the heart of the gang's business.[5] The U.S. Express worked with the American Express Company to serve Chicago, where American Express employed Allan Pinkerton as chief of security from 1856.[6] Latta was able to use this express network unmolested for fourteen years (1857–71).

Lonergan continues, "Latta was specially anxious to have his bail fixed at an amount he could give. I was willing he should go out on a small bail and his friends should think it was a small and trifling case." Latta's friends had a lot to fear from Lonergan's investigation. Pinkerton, a favorite of President Lincoln and the still-living William H. Seward, had made a name for himself around Chicago by "disrupting counterfeiters."[7] By the 1850s, Pinkerton's

Allan Pinkerton, President Abraham Lincoln and Major General John A. McClernand near Antietam, Maryland, on October 3, 1862. *Library of Congress.*

spy network overlapped Latta's criminal network between New York City and Chicago.[8] These Pinkerton spies, largely drawn from the likes of prostitutes and smugglers,[9] formed the cornerstone of the Scotsman's Chicago business and were the springboard for his lucrative Washington, D.C. work, including work for the Treasury when Latta was at his counterfeiting peak.[10] Lonergan knew these facts and continued his testimony with caution: "Latta offered to turn up all the parties engaged in the business, giving names of certain parties in this vicinity and two or more parties in New York."[11]

Unfortunately for Latta, Lonergan didn't want to hear about New York counterfeiters during Latta's initial interrogation. Lonergan *especially* didn't want to hear about Chicago counterfeiters. As head of the Chicago branch of the Secret Service, Lonergan had seized letters from Latta's Monroe house, which the *Chicago Tribune* described as "from a private detective in Chicago, who was acting, it would seem, as adviser, not only as to the movements of the government detectives, but as to the disposition of 'coney' [counterfeit money]."[12] Lonergan studiously failed to mention these letters in his Janesville testimony, despite acknowledging that Latta was "in some detective service" and that Latta had previously avoided sentencing on the strength of working with Allan Pinkerton.[13] During Latta's second 1872 trial, his lawyers described these Chicago letters as proving their client worked for the "secret service," but neither the letters nor Agent Lonergan could be found to testify again.[14]

During that summer of 1871, Lonergan wanted to hear only about "parties in the vicinity" of Green County, Wisconsin. Who exactly these "parties" were drew sniggers from the editor of the *Janesville Gazette* on the night before Lonergan's testimony. The editor noted that Monroe was "well represented" by the dignitaries summoned during the course of Latta's examination.

> *I then asked him* [Latta] *if he would tell me of any plates or counterfeit money concealed here* [in Green and Rock Counties] *and he then answered me there were none that he knew of; he said while he knew nothing of those matters here, he was aware of certain other matters of that character in the east and he went on to mention the names of certain parties who had plates....I recollect he asked me if I would rather have them than him.*[15]

For all his cunning, Latta seemed slow on the uptake regarding Detective Lonergan's highly localized investigative goals:

> [Lonergan]…*I think about that time I said I was satisfied there was considerable counterfeit material in this section* [Green County], *at that time I thought there were plates here. He said "You are mistaken so far as plates are concerned—there never has been one in this section and if there is any counterfeit money I don't know of it."…I think I closed the conversation by saying "if you want to talk at all, you had better talk the truth, that story is too old to impose on anybody." We may have been there five minutes or it may have been fifteen.…I have no recollection of stating to Latta that two or three years would be worth saving.*

Then the "truth" suddenly hit Latta:

> *The prisoner* [Latta] *stated at the jail on the morning of July 1st that the only counterfeit money, so far as he knew, in the vicinity of Monroe, was in the possession of Bill and John Watson.*

Lonergan testified that Latta gave him detailed directions for where to find the "Watson" money at the "old Dan Tuttle place"—buried under currant bushes in a "boot leg" and an "old keg."

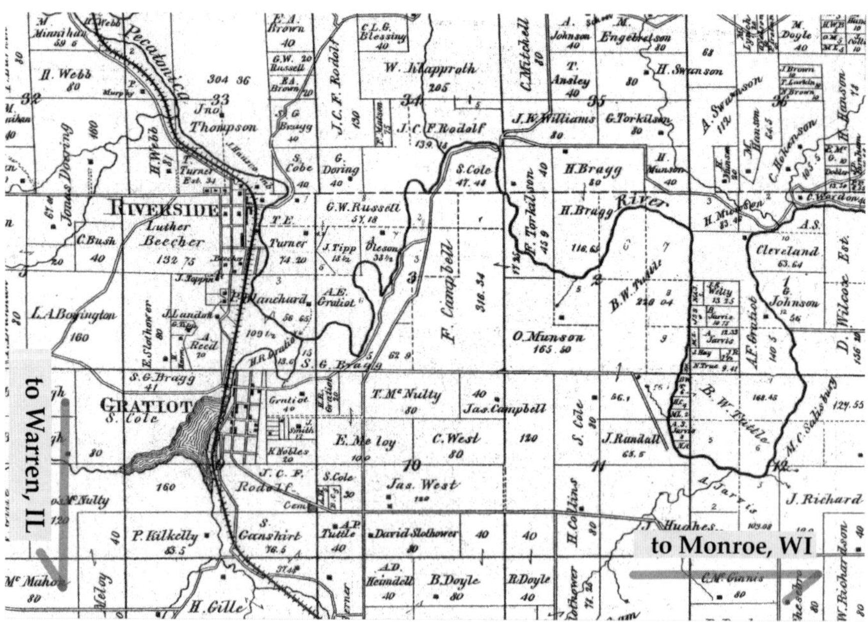

This image from the 1874 *Atlas of La Fayette County, Wisconsin* map of Gratiot shows Tuttle's land ("Old Dan Tuttle's place") surrounded by the Pecatonica River. *Argyle Public Library.*

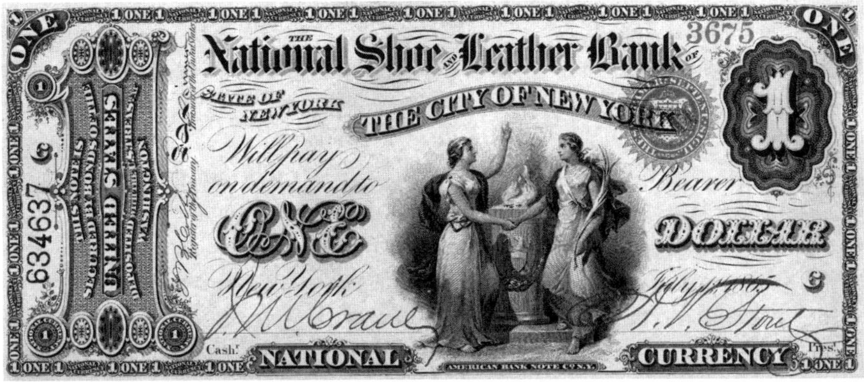

Top: Small-denomination bills were forged for Latta's contacts, for example: Front, $1 National Shoe Leather Bank of the City of New York, 1865. *American Numismatic Association.*

Bottom: Reverse side of the 1865 $1 National Shoe Leather Bank bill. Their moral failings aside, the artistry of Latta's counterfeiters was breathtaking. *American Numismatic Association.*

Latta was able to rattle off the names and denominations of the bills that Operative Lonergan would dig up: $15,000 total, $1,000 of which was $10 bills from the Farmer's & Mechanic's Bank of Poughkeepsie, New York, and the balance in $20 bills from various New York national banks. The real identity of the "Watsons" goes some way to explaining why these were all New York banks.

While testifying, Lonergan appeared unaware that "John Watson" and "William Watson" were aliases for two of the highly gifted New York Ballard brothers. These English brothers numbered at least three in total, and their real names were Thomas, George and John.[16] The "Watson"/Ballard brothers ran a node of the Bonelatta Gang distribution system out of a farm at Clear Lake, Iowa, and a large printing operation on Rivington Street in

New York City in addition to their Gratiot, Wisconsin farm. While John Ballard was arrested that July day by Lonergan near Monroe, his brother Tom was still at liberty out east.

Tom Ballard was one of the best currency plate engravers in the nation: he worked on the United States "greenback" bills for Salmon P. Chase[17] and moonlighted for Joshua D. Miner, a New York City gangster and politician. In a few months' time, Tom Ballard would be key witness for the Bonelatta Gang prosecutions in New York City, where Lonergan's boss Colonel Hiram Whitley had jurisdiction.

The result of Lonergan's testimony in Janesville was that Bone Latta was indicted at La Crosse, Wisconsin, in mid-September 1871. During the indictment hearings, John Sherman was mysteriously swapped with another Monroe man named George Thrall, for whom Arabut Ludlow personally paid bail.[18] This switch came with violence: Monroe's Deputy Marshal A.J. High had his home burned by arsonists[19] who threatened him if he cooperated in the counterfeiting case.[20] Arson was a classic Banditti tactic. As the flames rose, many Monroe residents refused to help, either from fear or in solidarity with the criminals. The hypocrisy of Ludlow and his friends is reflected in their behavior: while the Bonelatta arsonists terrorized Ludlow's neighbors, his church booked Sojourner Truth to lecture on the plight of Blacks in Washington.[21]

Despite the violence in Monroe, Latta's trial began on February 26, 1872, and continued through June. Latta enjoyed first-class legal representation throughout his ordeal. No less than Charles G. Williams, a Wisconsin state senator, volunteered to defend him. Senator Williams was by birth a New Yorker who represented Janesville and the surrounding area.[22]

Wisconsin State Senator Charles G. Williams (1869–73), who became a congressman in Washington, D.C. (1873–83). *Collection of the U.S. House of Representatives.*

Williams was not a hardscrabble political outsider: he served as *pro tempore* president of the Wisconsin Senate at the time of Latta's trial. Williams was an ambitious Republican on the warpath for a congressional seat in Washington, D.C., which he won a few months later. He had been an elector for President Grant in 1868.

Throughout the trial, Williams waxed poetic on Latta's behalf, but a cataclysmic prosecution for the New York branch of Latta's gang had

Section of reverse face, $100 "greenback" issued by the U.S. Treasury after 1863 via the American Bank Note Company, New York. *American Numismatic Association.*

taken place in the meantime and this churned up more evidence against Latta. Monroe's favorite counterfeiter went into that June 1872 courtroom under a great pall, but with the Republican establishment holding his hand.

Everything was in Latta's favor, except perhaps for the evidence and public opinion outside of Green County. On June 21, 1872, Latta was convicted of counterfeiting and sentenced to ten years' imprisonment. (That's five years *less* than what the reverse of Lincoln's greenback notes say he should have gotten.) *The Wisconsin State Journal* celebrated this outcome:

> *The result of the trial, in the face of the pressure brought to bear by Mr. Latta's friends on his behalf, and against the principal Government witness, and confident assertions that conviction was impossible, is the best evidence of their* [the prosecuting lawyers'] *efficiency on behalf of the Government.*

So ended Operative Lonergan's involvement with that network of provincial criminals and their powerful friends. Who could blame the Secret Service agent's courtroom fear? He hardly expected to kick a political wasps' nest way out in southern Wisconsin. His dithering 1871 testimony belies the fact that he had started the Latta investigation with ruthless efficiency the previous winter.

In February 1871, half a year before Chicago's Great Fire, Thomas E. Lonergan, chief operative of the U.S. Secret Service in that city, began investigating a gang of counterfeiters "whose existence had for years been suspected."[23] In years prior, anti-counterfeiting work had been the forte of the Pinkerton Detective Agency, an organization that acted as a private police force for wealthy industrialists, gambling dons and railway barons.[24] If Lonergan ever worked with the Pinkertons during his Bonelatta investigation, it was not reported by the newspapers. This is odd because both Lonergan and the Pinkertons were not shy about talking to the press. In addition, Allan Pinkerton was famous for his detailed files on active criminals.[25] Under normal circumstances, the Secret Service should have been eager to draw on the firm's experience.

Instead, press coverage focused on Lonergan's work with Chicago's official police: reports led Detective Lonergan to a ring operating out of Monroe, Wisconsin, which was headed by "Napoleon Bonaparte Latta." Latta traveled from Monroe to Chicago about once a month and commanded a corps of "shovers" who undertook the dangerous business of putting fake notes into circulation.

The Bonelatta Gang was well organized. Latta posted lookouts around Monroe's central Square, at the train station and outside the old mining town's many bars. Some gang members were tasked with befriending strangers in order to ferret out potential government agents. Lonergan wasn't just going to appear in Monroe and bag his man; in fact, he knew Latta's men would recognize his face on sight.[26] Therefore, he sent in a subordinate agent who was unknown to the gang and disguised as a traveling soap peddler.

This "peddler," an agent named Charley Anderson, was able to gain access to the heart of the ring. To do this, Anderson set up a makeshift sidewalk soap stand on the Square. Lonergan had boxes of soap transported to Anderson daily; the service purchased three different real estate lots around town in apparent anticipation of a more permanent premises; and Anderson even sought out local investors for a proposed store.[27] Anderson was such a good talker that he convinced Bone Latta himself of his veracity.

Anderson probably did a little more than just talk up his soap because he pinpointed not only the saloon headquarters where Latta did business but also the precise location inside that saloon so that he could eavesdrop from the adjacent building. Supposedly, Anderson was always able to scurry back to his street corner soap stand before he was noticed. In reality, Anderson probably gained his information by asking to buy counterfeit bills at some point. It was a common practice for unethical merchants to give change in bad bills.[28] It took Anderson three weeks to establish the confidence of the Bonelatta Gang.

The information Anderson gained was enlightening. Latta's "hand off" procedure employed cohorts of men who escorted buyers around the county.[29] The gang's clients, who were purchasers of large amounts of counterfeit currency, would travel by train to Monroe, where "certain parties" would meet them at the station and escort them about ten miles into the country. There the buyers would meet another "party traveling with a team" and be ready to pay 20 to 45 cents on the face-note dollar value for fake money. The trade was made quietly at the roadside, and the buyers would turn around and head back to Monroe, while the sellers went off in a different direction.

When buyers were trusted, Latta's gang would send wads of bills through the local express company (U.S. Express). Lonergan had intercepted a number of these express packages. What Latta was conducting was the express company variant of the "green goods game,"[30] traditionally a postal service–based counterfeit currency scam, which was well-known to law enforcement by the 1870s.

Lonergan didn't personally come to Monroe until Thursday, June 29, when enough evidence had been found to make arrests. Even at that time, it was too dangerous for him to ride the train directly into town; he had to disembark several miles before Monroe and didn't arrive before 9:00 p.m. The men accompanying Lonergan included his Secret Service colleague John Egan out of St. Louis, Missouri; one "Deputy U.S. Marshal Comstock"; and Rock County (Janesville) Sheriff R.T. Pember. Conspicuously absent were Green County (Monroe) Sheriff Alfred Wood and Deputy Marshal (soon sheriff) A.J. High, who would only join in assisting the arrests later.

The Bonelatta men were not held in Monroe long, just one night, and then they were whisked to Janesville on the 5:30 p.m. train. Latta was released on bail paid by anonymous friends and pledged to appear before the examiners at Janesville on July 28.

Arrests did not stop there. On the night of July 2, William H. Watson was apprehended. On July 5, an additional two men were "taken in their beds" by Lonergan: prominent Monroe hotel owners Robert Allensworth of the American House and Casper Oswold of the Monroe House. Bone Latta was *re*-arrested on three additional charges at the same time.

As regards to these new charges against Latta, the *Daily Gazette* of July 6 said:

> *Latta is regarded as the head center of that class of rascals in Wisconsin and Northern Illinois, but his operations have not been confined to any particular district.*

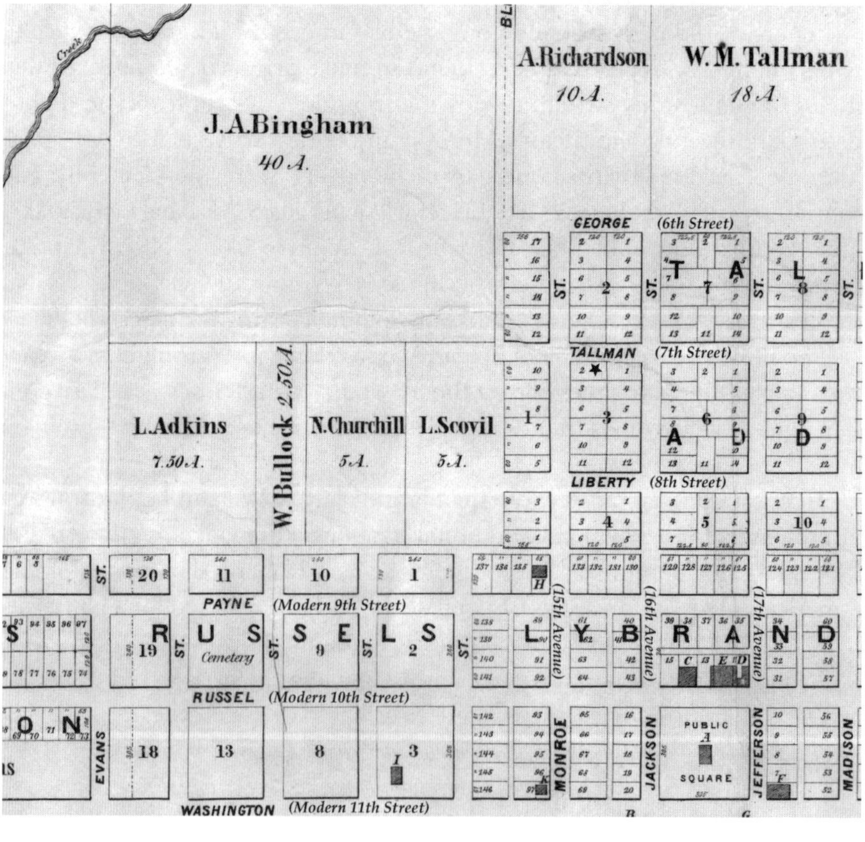

Creek
J.A.Bingham
40 A.
A.Richardson
10 A.
W.M.Tallman
18 A.
L.Adkins
7.50 A.
W. Bullock 2.50 A.
N.Churchill
5 A.
L.Scovil
5 A.
GEORGE (6th Street)
TALLMAN (7th Street)
LIBERTY (8th Street)
PAYNE (Modern 9th Street)
RUSSEL (Modern 10th Street)
WASHINGTON (Modern 11th Street)
(15th Avenue)
(16th Avenue)
(17th Avenue)
EVANS
MONROE
JACKSON
JEFFERSON
MADISON
TALLMAN ADD
RUSSELS
LYBRAND
Cemetery
PUBLIC SQUARE

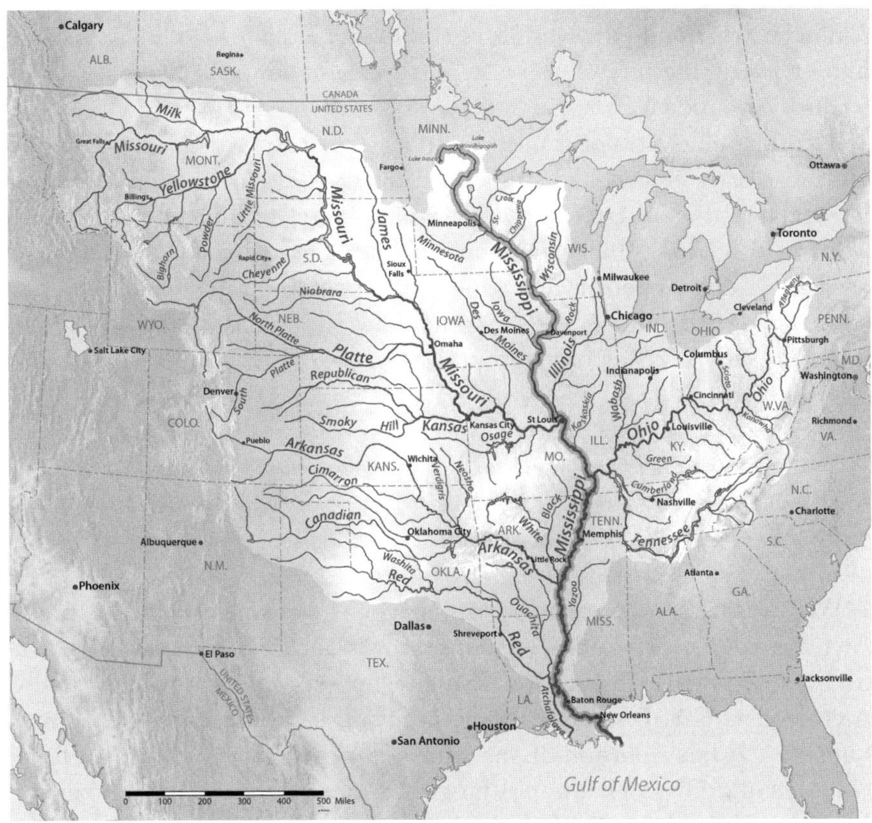

Opposite, top: This lost "Konac Inn" Monroe building may have been Latta's residence. "Coniack," a corruption of cognac, was nineteenth-century slang for counterfeit currency. *Author's collection.*

Opposite, bottom: Latta's residence was probably on Fifteenth Avenue, between Seventh and Eighth Streets. His neighbor Sam Boynton's home is marked with a star. *Wisconsin Historical Society.*

Above: A map of the Mississippi River Basin. *Wikipedia, © Shannon1 CC BY-SA 4.0.*

In fact, Latta's distribution network covered the Mississippi River Basin through Texas and on into Mexico. The Midwestern states of Michigan, Minnesota, Kansas, Wisconsin, Illinois, Indiana, Iowa and the key financial hub Missouri were all afflicted.

Lonergan's prominent July arrests were bad enough, but then the unthinkable happened: when Latta returned to Monroe by train, having been bailed from his second arrest, a royal welcome awaited him. Village board members had paid the Monroe Brass Band to serenade Latta on the platform. Two hundred townsfolk assembled at the station to either celebrate him or just to see him. This boisterous welcome for a likely counterfeiter terrified Monroe's leaders.

Monroe's elite did not want continuing Treasury investigations. By July 19, the *Monroe Sentinel* had printed an alleged statement from Detective Lonergan to the *Chicago Times* that five out of twelve Monroe citizens were working with Latta.[31] In fact it is doubtful that Lonergan made the statement at all: Operative Anderson even wrote to the *Sentinel* denying that his superior would say such a thing.[32] The "five out of twelve" rumor is likely a garbled version of this July 3 reporting from the *Chicago Tribune*:

> *About a dozen of the citizens of Monroe were connected with them* [Latta and John Sherman], *two or three being prominent businessmen. It was not considered expedient to arrest them, as they can be secured at almost any time. They will probably be used as witnesses.*[33]

Who were these prominent businessmen? Fortunately, the National Archives in Chicago does contain records for Bone Latta's series of trials,[34] and the prominent Monroe men who were called as witnesses were A.C. Dodge, C.S. Foster, H. Howe, J.F. Pool, E. Bartlett and Charlton J. Simmons. A large portion of the witnesses subpoenaed were part of the "Home Guard," a vigilante pro-Lincoln group, or they were members of Monroe's Universalist Church. If these men were victims of Bone Latta, neither the *Sentinel* nor the village board would have supported the gang. Rather, these men were part of Monroe's business elite who orbited the banker Arabut Ludlow.

2

LINCOLN, ABOLITION AND UNIVERSALISM

Latta's Supporters in Monroe, Wisconsin

In the 1850s, Monroe was an agricultural village rising from the ashes of a tumultuous mining past. On one hand, it was a town of saloons and their accompanying social difficulties. On the other, it was headquarters for an entrepreneurial clique of people who shared membership in the new Republican Party and Universalist Church.

The Republican Party was born in the town of Friendship in Allegany County, New York. The town was home to the *Genesee Valley Free Press*, the "Pioneer Republican Journal of America," and its editor A.N. Cole, to whom Horace Greeley suggested the party name "Republican."[1]

The party had a second home in Monroe, Wisconsin. From the 1850s to the 1870s, the most influential businesspeople were ardent Republicans. John Augustine Bingham was part of the national convention that renominated Lincoln in 1864;[2] banker Arabut Ludlow was a representative to the 1872 convention that renominated President Grant.[3] Bingham's mother-in-law, Almira Humes, the crotchety owner of the local whiskey hotel,[4] was partisan to the point of naming her lapdog after the defeated Samuel Tilden.[5]

In harmony with the party's foundation, many of Monroe's leaders were also abolitionists—up to a point. Most Wisconsin banks in Ludlow's era bought Southern, especially Missourian, bank securities because they were among the few available investments that were responsibly managed.[6] Being abolitionist did not necessarily go along with a desire for racial equality, either. For example, two of Ludlow's right-hand men, Nathan C. Twining and Daniel S. Young, organized a mutual benefit society called the Royal Arcanum, which was for Caucasian men only.[7] Abolition among this set was more about politics than ethics, and few had personal experience of the American South.

Besides Republican Party gatherings, Monroe's Universalist Church was a favorite venue for airing this type of abolitionist sentiment. Universalism shares a fascinating history with Unitarianism, and the two denominations are now joined. They both have roots in the conflict between the Holy Roman Empire and its Muslim Ottoman neighbor.[8] Rich border lords from the Bohemian Crown Lands wanted to trade with the Ottomans—trade in European slaves particularly[9]—despite Hapsburg opposition. This Bohemian elite bucked Hapsburg pressure with the help of Muslim slave-soldiers.[10] The resulting religious compromises gave birth to Unitarianism (denial of the Holy Trinity),[11] which found its way to British Civil War thinkers during the formation of the "New Model Army."[12] At the same time in London, religious radicals were interested in Universalism (the belief that everyone will be saved), an outgrowth of the occult writings of Jakob Böhme and radical Pietism.[13] Böhme's Hermeticism and Pietism both drew on occult traditions preserved in the Islamic world.[14] Therefore, Unitarianism and Universalism were red threads intertwined throughout England's radical ferment.

Members of Cromwell's new army, who were characterized by devotion to a Muhammad-like leader rather than a community or hereditary nobleman,[15] were encouraged to follow radical ("Independent") religiopolitical belief systems[16] (e.g., Levellers, Diggers, to a lesser extent Quakerism) as long as they were loyal or useful to Oliver Cromwell. Through Radical Protestantism, the English military tradition took on a decidedly Ottoman flavor.

Universalism found its way to Monroe, Wisconsin, in 1859 through New England families: the Ludlows, Binghams, Treats, Fosters and Richardsons.[17] They organized a diverse group of Protestants into a congregation under a strident abolitionist minister[18] who was succeeded by Zadok H. Howe. This church's financial backers feature prominently in the Bonelatta scandal: Arabut Ludlow and family; Norman Churchill, his mother, Almira Humes, and in-law John A. Bingham;[19] Joseph T. Dodge (his brother was Adam Clarke "A.C." Dodge);[20] Charles Stuart "C.S." Foster; and finally Asa Richardson.[21]

There were Universalists who had no connection with Bone Latta. There were also (likely) Latta men who were not openly Universalist like Samuel Elbert Miner, a lapsed Congregationalist minister.[22]

Left: Portrait of Almira Humes Churchill Robertson. This image was carried by her son, Charles Robertson, through his Civil War service. *Green County Historical Society.*

Right: Portrait of Caroline Churchill Bingham, Almira Humes's daughter and wife of John A. Bingham. *Green County Historical Society.*

The Universalist abolitionist Republicans were a tight social clique, and it's worth describing some of their business and family relationships. For example, the wives of J.V. Richardson and Arabut Ludlow were sisters or stepsisters.[23] Norman Churchill was the business partner of A.C. Dodge through their joint ownership of the local sawmill.[24] Bingham went into banking with Arabut Ludlow, to whom everyone owed money at some point.

Almira Humes is the only woman of standing in this group, and her wealth belies a tragic early history. Almira owned a hotel with a whiskey bar.[25] For those versed in nineteenth-century Midwestern crime history,[26] this confluence of businesses strongly suggests that prostitution was also practiced on the premises. Almira bought the bar from its founder Joseph Payne using funds that are hard to explain.

Prior to relocating to Monroe, Almira's life was one of desperate poverty, abuse and marital nonconformity.[27] Immediately upon settling in Monroe, Almira opened a "boarding house," a common euphemism for a bordello.[28] We will never be able to confirm or disprove Almira's participation in the sex trade because Green County's criminal case files have gone missing. After just a few years running the "boarding house," Almira Humes bought Payne's upmarket whiskey hotel.

Almira attracted Green County's most ambitious men. John A. Bingham was a schoolteacher when he came to Monroe, registered at Almira's and eventually married Almira's daughter Caroline.[29] It seems likely that Almira's earnings at least partially financed his banking endeavors with Arabut Ludlow.

Almira Humes's early life was tragic, but few people in town knew how tragic before her granddaughter Dr. Helen Bingham wrote a revealing obituary for her in the local paper.[30] Almira Humes was born in 1806 in Portsmouth, New Hampshire, to a fanatical disciple of "Thomsonian Medicine" named Huldah Temple Humes. Huldah made herself sick on Thomson's herbal "cures" so often that preteen Almira had to parent the household. Almira's biological father died when she was a few years old, and what little parental care Almira received came from her stepfather, Silas Gardner. Helen tried to explain her grandmother's bitter demeanor:

> *Some of this severe mien, Dr. Bingham wrote, could be traced to an ordeal of early childhood when her mother, Hulda, fearing death was near [having overdosed], gave her daughter to a couple recommended as pious. The little girl, then about eight, was gone a year when her stepfather traced her down upon hearing that she was being treated cruelly and worked like a slave. He returned her to the family fold but the scars of her experience remained in mind for life. Dire circumstances of her years in Illinois also extracted their toll.*[31]

We are not told what these "dire" Illinois experiences were; however, circumstances may provide a clue. Huldah, and her equally odd sisters Nabby and Naomi, had taken the family on a nearly four-year exodus from New Hampshire to Illinois via the Allegheny and Ohio Rivers. The trio, whom Almira described as "very proud" so that "any one of them would be willing to be queen," adopted more children and indigents along the way, which taxed their already meager resources. Silas Gardner, the only spouse to accompany the trio, tried to support them all by shoemaking but died along the journey.[32] Almira was left to scrounge a living

Almira Humes in later life. *Green County Historical Society.*

in riverbank settlements like Cincinnati. Without money or a competent guardian, the options for a friendless teen girl were few. Almira represented the typical demographic exploited by nineteenth-century pimps.

At some time during this Illinois stay, Almira "married" a man named William Boardman Churchill,[33] whom Monroe historian E.C. Hamilton described as "a poor manager or hard-luck provider."[34] Almira left William in 1840 when she was thirty-four years old, which was typically the end of nineteenth-century prostitute's marketable life.[35] Almira had five children while with William, and she took them all, along with her mother, northward to Monroe, where she started her "boarding house." Where the money for this endeavor came from is unclear. Almira did have a brother in Galena, Illinois, and another somewhere "in the vicinity" of Monroe mining lead, but there is no evidence that they helped her.

To what sort of town had Almira fled with her family? Neither Galena nor Monroe attracted a nice group of people. They were both mining towns with a saloon culture.[36] Here is a description of Galena by H.F. Kett and Company:

> *Thousands of rough miners swarmed through her streets. All sorts of moving vehicles were seen in her thoroughfares, and every language was spoken, every costume worn. The miner generally spent all he made, was poor, and held his own remarkably well. And that reckless spirit, bred of all uncertain pursuits, was abundantly manifested among the miners who assembled in the lead regions. Card playing and whiskey drinking, quarreling, and that rough desperate life developed among adventurers of all classes gathered about Galena, was characteristic of those of all other mines.*[37]

This was the milieu in which thirty-four-year-old Almira sought to support herself, her incompetent mother and five children.

While most miners died poor, Galena, Illinois, was good to President Ulysses S. Grant, and this area was his political home base.[38] A handful of merchants became wealthy from Galena's mineral boom, and they formed the core of Grant's political support. These merchants followed Grant to Washington, D.C.

Grant's Galena men would have known about the counterfeit money gushing from the eastern edge of the precious lead deposits. One of the first actions Grant's Treasury took was to break up Monroe's Bonelatta Gang with the new and dubiously staffed Secret Service.[39] While the gang's operations were ended, most gang members faced no legal consequences.

(Arabut Ludlow, as owner of a national bank, had underwritten Lincoln's war effort, which was the source of Grant's political success.)

Almira's 1840s clientele were probably not tony like the Grant-affiliated merchants described previously, but her establishment prospered to the point where she was able to buy Joseph Payne's hotel.[40] This was an astounding financial feat: Payne had to flee town in 1850,[41] so Almira raised this capital in at most ten years while presumably paying rent or paying off the construction of her first inn and raising a family of five.

Almira continued the success of Payne's "whiskey hotel," but marital troubles pursued her:

> *In September 1843, Almira, having convinced William Churchill there could be no reconciliation, was married to Jesse Robertson, 13 years her junior….Almira and Robertson were separated in 1878 and he later obtained a divorce.*[42]

No record of Almira's marriage to or divorce from William Churchill is known, and the arrangement described sounds informal. Unofficial marriages or changing husbands (outside of widowhood) were rare during Almira's time, except for women involved in the commercial sex industry, where such flexible arrangements were common. Almira Humes's bitter demeanor does become understandable in light of the trials she suffered.

About a month after Almira married Jesse (which is documented), her daughter Caroline Churchill married John Augustine Bingham. Bingham was then practicing law but would later run a "currency exchange" on the advice of Ohio congressman Columbus Delano.[43] Much of Bingham's business came from the Milwaukee & Mississippi Railway Company. He and Ludlow rolled this exchange into a bank to help finance the M&M Railroad extension through Monroe. In May 1856, the pair's Bank of Monroe was organized according to state laws.

The cashier of Ludlow and Bingham's bank was J.B. Galusha, who was picked by that same Ohio congressman Columbus Delano.[44] At this time, Delano was in between his first (1845–47) and second (1865–67) congressional terms and was living in Monroe as an agent for the M&M Railroad, the bank's leading client. Although from a prominent family, Delano himself was not wealthy until he set up a Wall Street banking outfit named Delano, Dunlevy, & Company, which was in operation by 1852.[45] Delano was a "zealous" supporter of Abraham Lincoln[46] as well as a cousin to Ulysses S. Grant.[47] He owned land around Monroe by 1861.[48]

Left: John Augustine Bingham became Green County's judge in 1849 and served one decade. *Green County Historical Society.*

Right: Portrait of Columbus Delano, three-time representative of Ohio in Washington D.C. *Library of Congress.*

Banking House of

DUNLEVY, DELANO & CO.

34 West Third Street, Cincinnati,

Buy and sell exchanges on New York, Philadelphia, and the principal cities of the Unitee States. Discounts good business paper at low rates. Allow interest on deposites.

This House is connected with the House of Delano, Dunlevy, & Co., 39, Wall street, New York, who buy and sell railroad stock, city and county bonds, and other securities on commission. Also keep accounts for Western banks and brokers, and allow nterest on the same. july—tf

Dunlevy, Delano & Co. ad in *The Western Star* of Lebanon, OH, January 9, 1852. In 1858, Monroe had just incorporated, enabling men like Delano to lend the town money.

The Bingham-Ludlow partnership was fraught. It was Bingham's acumen that led to establishing the National Bank of Monroe in 1864, though within a year Asa Richardson and Ludlow became sole proprietors after the trio quarreled.[49] Bingham died months later, while Ludlow's bank prospered as one of the First National Bank of Chicago's earliest banking clients.[50]

It is interesting that Ludlow and Bingham would organize their bank and finance their rail extension in the months prior to Napoleon Bonaparte Latta's transition to Monroe. It was the M&M's arrival in Monroe that opened the town to Latta's lucrative express package strategy, and Ludlow's bank thrived under these seemingly adverse conditions. Latta never counterfeited Ludlow banknotes.

How influential were Ludlow's Republican abolitionist Universalist crew in Monroe? It's difficult to find an area of village life that they didn't manage. Ludlow organized the county agricultural fair, and its board positions would rotate between prominent universalists or their friends, including Fred F. West.[51] West served as sheriff in the 1840s and supported Bone Latta in 1871.[52]

Ludlow was also a social leader. In keeping with his Protestant New England background, he was a charting founder of Monroe's Sons of Temperance society in 1848. Other charter members included his Universalist chums J.V. Richardson and Charles S. Foster, as well as Fred West.[53]

Finally, Ludlow's clique enjoyed leadership of the local government. To list all their positions would be awkward, but suffice it to say that Fred West was on the Green County Board by 1854 and held his first Monroe "city" board position by 1859.[54] By 1870, the city board included a shadowy politician named Dr. Lucien B. Johnson. Johnson joined West in public support of Latta[55] and served on the board a couple times *after* the scandal.

Dr. Johnson is Monroe, Wisconsin's connection with the early Republican Party in Friendship, New York. Johnson was a politician in that very Allegany County where the party was born: he was elected to the state assembly on the first ballot Republicans ran candidates.[56] Johnson's political career was short, and he moved to Monroe swiftly afterward.[57] The problem, readers, came from the actions of William H. Seward, Pinkerton partisan and abolitionist extraordinaire.

In 1854, the people of Allegany County, New York, elected Dr. Lucien B. Johnson and Lucius S. May as their assemblymen. At this time, "Republican" party politics were closely associated with *New York Tribune* editor Horace Greeley, who supported William H. Seward. Everything was going well for Dr. Johnson.

Right: John A. Bingham with his daughter, Helen, who became a homeopathic doctor and Green County historian. *Green County Historical Society.*

Below: Signatures from Napoleon Bonaparte Latta and Dr. Lucien B. Johnson on Latta's bail of February 29, 1872. *National Archives, Chicago.*

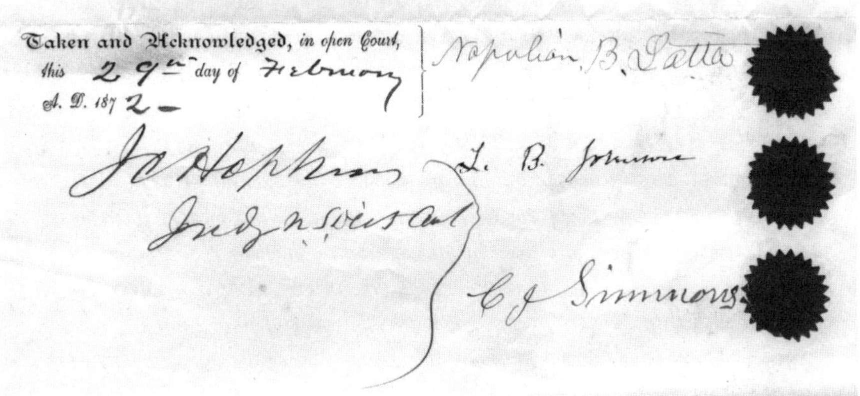

Taken and Acknowledged, *in open Court, this* 29th *day of* February *A. D. 187*2 —

Napolion B. Latta

J C Hopkins

L. B. Johnson

C J Simmons

By February 1855, however, the *Hornellsville Weekly Tribune* reported that Dr. Johnson had been burned in effigy outside the Albany legislature alongside Speaker DeWitt C. Littlejohn.[58] Most reports state that a "Dr. Thomspon" was burned instead of Dr. Johnson, but the true matter at hand closely affected Johnson's legislative colleague Lucius S. May[59] and, therefore, probably shortened Johnson's political career in Allegany too.

The burning was a result of certain representatives, including Littlejohn and May, voting for Seward after having given an oath to their "Know Nothing" constituents not to do so.[60] The Know Nothings were a recently founded party dedicated to protecting the interests of working Americans from the great landowners and industrialists who sought to import cheap labor. By supporting Seward, Littlejohn and May had betrayed their constituents.

As a result, Seward became known for dishonorable tactics, the political debate became "spicy" and Dr. Johnson got out of New York.[61] By 1857, he had settled in Monroe, Wisconsin, and befriended all the right people. Johnson's earlier dealings with Seward's machine go some way in explaining the doctor's support for Lincoln's counterfeiter Bone Latta in 1871.

Here we come to a dark side of Monroe's politics, because Ludlow's clique was not toothless. In 1862, when Lincoln's unpopular war was not going well for the Union, the clique organized a band of vigilantes to assault any Monroe resident they felt didn't support their pro-Lincoln cause. (Pro-Union wasn't enough!) This band would intimidate residents into signing loyalty oaths designed by one of the clique's special committees. Dr. Johnson was one of these thought police, as were Arabut Ludlow, A.C. Dodge, C.S. Foster, Joseph Pool, Edmund Bartlett, John A. Bingham, George Churchill (one of Almira's sons) and Josiah V. Richardson (banker Asa's son).[62]

The Home Guard vigilante crew was birthed at a July 1862 meeting at the courthouse on the Square. The motivation for the Guard is explained by an excerpt from the *Monroe Sentinel*, as reprinted in the 1884 History:

> *COURT HOUSE, MONROE, July 28* [1862]
> *A traitor having been sentenced this afternoon, to five weeks imprisonment for kicking and otherwise abusing a sick and discharged soldier for the expression of Union sentiments, his secession friends said he should not go to jail, and if he did 100 men from the county would liberate him. Whereupon a general fight ensued in which "secesh" got much the worst of it—a meeting was called of the loyal citizens to be held at the court house, which was organized by calling the Hon. F.H. West* [Francis H. West, Green County state senator] *to the chair and appointing A. W. Potter, secretary.*[63]

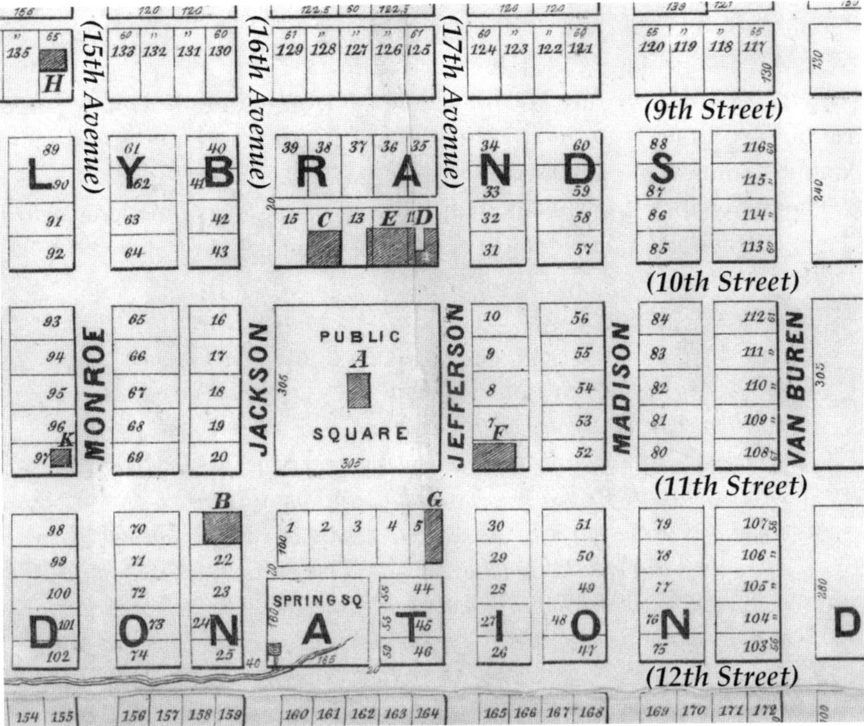

This 1857 map shows Monroe's Courthouse Square. Building *E* is Ludlow's bank. *C* is the "Monroe" hotel; *D* is the "United States" and *B* is the American. *Wisconsin Historical Society.*

As it turns out, the fight that motivated this meeting was actually between two Union men and it wasn't about secession. One party had criticized "the present administration"[64]—that is, the Lincoln administration—which led to the brawl.

The stated object of the July meeting was the suppression of "home rebels." Josiah V. Richardson was among attendees who drew up incendiary resolutions such as "Whereas, the hydra-headed demon of secession is again moving in our midst and exerting a paralyzing influence upon the cause" and called on his followers to "discountenance in every possible manner all exhibits of treason."

The meeting's next action was to create a "military company" that would "mete out to traitors the punishment they so justly deserve." Members of this company included the luminaries of the Universalist Church and many of the local men called to testify for the Latta trial in 1872: George Churchill, N.B. Treat, Allen Woodle, J.C. Scoville, Edmund Bartlett,

Joseph Pool, Harris Pool, George E. Thrall, H.W. Whitney, Francis H. West, A.C. Dodge, Dr. L.B. Johnson, Charles S. Foster, John A. Bingham, J.V. Richardson and Brooks Dunwiddie.[65] George Thrall actually stood trial next to Bone Latta in 1872. Dr. Johnson had paid Latta's bail, while Arabut Ludlow had paid Thrall's.

These vigilantes took it upon themselves to enforce something called "Pope's Order No. 3, Headquarters Army of Virginia," from July 23, 1862, which stated:

> *Commanders of army corps, divisions, brigades, and detached commands will proceed immediately to arrest disloyal male citizens, within their lines or within their reach, and within their respective stations. Such as are willing to take the oath of allegiance to the United States and will furnish sufficient security for its observance, shall be permitted to remain at their homes and pursue in good faith their accustomed avocations. Those who refuse shall be conducted to the south beyond the extreme pickets of this army, and be notified that if found again anywhere within our lines; or at any point in the rear, they will be considered as spies, and subjected to the extreme rigor of military law. If any person having taken the oath of allegiance as above specified shall be found to have violated it, he shall be shot, and his property seized and confiscated."**
>
> **The oath, before mentioned, was given into the possession of L. Rote, an attorney and justice of the peace. A large number of citizens made haste to subscribe their names to it; indeed, there were but few that refused to sign. Of the latter, one was a resident of the town of Sylvester, an old time citizen; he was marched to the limits of the village of Monroe, and ordered to keep outside. A resident of Clarno was treated to a free ride on a rail part of the way to his home.—Editor.*[66]

Being "rode out of town on a rail" was a form of torture. The victim was made to straddle a fence rail held on the shoulders of other men, who then paraded the victim or took him to the city limits. Helen Bingham records that one man railed was a Mr. Steves of Durand, who sued Lewis Rote and other Monroe men for assault in a Milwaukee court in 1865. Mr. Steves was awarded $5,000 damages.[67] (Helen Bingham doesn't name the other defendants—unsurprising given her father's involvement.)

Things didn't stop with Mr. Steves. A special judicial committee—Monroe's leaders loved committees—was set up to investigate anyone who refused to take the oath. These "judges" were Benjamin Chenoweth, N.R. Usher, Charles S. Foster, John A. Bingham, Josiah V. Richardson, L. Davenport, D.W. Ball, Brooks Dunwiddie and Arabut Ludlow.[68] During the following months, Green County earned a reputation for mob violence among the county's critics in the state capital.[69]

The scars the Civil War left on Monroe, Wisconsin, as a community ran very deep. Green County historian Jonathon Rupp recalled how families avoided talking about that time.[70] Parents and grandparents may have *made up* stories about meeting American Indians in their backyard, but no amount of cajoling from their children could induce them to speak or write about that fratricidal conflict. Arabut Ludlow and his followers have more than a little for which to answer.

3

INDIGNATION AND MONROE'S MINER FAMILY

In Monroe, Wisconsin, the trauma of the Civil War left a group of people in power who believed that their ends justified their means. This same group sweated profusely when they thought Secret Service Operative Lonergan had said that *five out of twelve* of Monroe's residents were Bonelatta Gang confederates. Monroe's newspaper editors did not pause to verify Lonergan's statement—they simply presumed it was true. Such an unforced error might be indicative of a bad conscience.

The appearance of the Monroe Bass Band at Latta's homecoming did little to dispel the notion that 42 percent of Monroe was rotten. Not only did Lonergan's alleged public statements suggest further investigations, but politicians like Fred F. West and Dr. Lucien B. Johnson were fanning the flames of justice by celebrating the chief culprit (or sacrificial lamb) Bone Latta as well. This was too much for the elite of Monroe. Something would have to be done, and it would be done by committee.

On the evening of Monday, August 4, 1871, an "Indignation Meeting" was organized at Union Hall by Universalist minister Zedok H. Howe.[1] The purpose of the meeting was to decide how to deal with the publicity that resulted from the actions of village board members who had paid the band to serenade Latta on his return from examination in Janesville.

This meeting comprised leading men of the village, men who had built Monroe three decades before. Chief among these was Norman Churchill (Almira Humes's son) and Benjamin Chenoweth. Chenoweth was a

Portrait of Universalist minister, ink and paper merchant and Ludlow functionary Zadok Howe. *Green County Historical Society*.

director of Ludlow's bank[2] and served on the village board multiple times.[3] Fred West asked both Chenoweth and Churchill to chair the "Indignation Meeting" but both declined. Samuel Elbert Miner, a probable counterfeiting family member, was appointed chairman instead.

The meeting kicked off with a motion to establish a committee who would report resolutions to the public. Fred West wanted to avoid this, but the other meeting leaders carried it, and the following committee of "reporters" was formed: H.W. Whitney, A.C. Dodge, Charles Foster, D.B. Davenport and Zadok H. Howe. Readers will recognize those names from the "judicial committee" and "military company" of the Home Guard vigilantes.

Howe stated that the committee's main concern were those "newspaper reports" that Detective Lonergan was alleged to have made. Committeemen were eager to discredit this five out of twelve claim. They also wanted to distance themselves from the actions of "village board members" who had both bailed out Latta and paid for his serenade. To kill two birds with one stone, the board chose to promote a misleading notion that "all the other citizens had been cleared and discharged" besides Latta. (This was not true. The men beyond Sherman and Latta were discharged but not cleared of wrongdoing. Casper Oswald, the U.S. House hotelier, would in a month's time be rearrested in Fond du Lac for circulating a great deal more counterfeit currency.[4] George Thrall of Monroe, a banknote dealer,[5] would be also charged with Latta around that time and later found guilty.[6])

The language used by the reporting committee was similar to that used by the *Monroe Sentinel* editors from the start of the scandal. The *Sentinel* editors' attitude toward the scandal was strange.[7] When Latta was first arrested and the scope of the economic devastation he wreaked initially comprehended, the most the *Sentinel* could do was complain that *Chicago Tribune* reporting had placed the Pecatonica River too near Monroe's city limits.[8] *Sentinel* writers heaped scorn on Lonergan and his investigation as a "*first-class* sensation," insinuating *ex ante* that all charges were probably trumped up.[9] They even unflatteringly compared Lonergan to a dog. The wisdom of such an editorial policy, from a paper printed in Arabut Ludlow's bank building on the Square,[10] appears never to have been considered. It's not surprising therefore that Fred West and Dr. Johnson thought they were safe with their musical antics.

Portrait of Norman Churchill, town heavyweight and Almira Humes's son. *Green County Historical Society.*

During the course of the "Indignation" meeting, it became clear that townsfolk knew who on the village board were Bone Latta's benefactors. Watchmaker Sam B. Boynton, a neighbor of Latta[11] who would be called to testify on the last days of Latta's Madison trial, pointed out that only Fred West seemed "excited" at the prospect of the committee. Boynton was also a precious metals dealer and therefore a likely target for counterfeit shovers. Boynton added that "it had been three days since the band had been hired by Doctor Johnson to go to the depot and serenade N. B. Latta," At this, Dr. Johnson jumped up and flatly accused Boynton of lying. Boynton shot back that the exact price of the serenade was $10. Whatever the veracity of Boynton's claim, by September 20 the *Sentinel* would print that L.B. Johnson and Fred West paid Latta's $8,000 bail in Janesville.[12]

The details of the bail could not be openly admitted during the "Indignation Meeting," however. As Boynton, Johnson and West thrust at one another, Sam Miner quieted the din and, as the chairman of the meeting, began to make pronouncements. Miner didn't want Boynton to vent "personal issues" around the "misfortune of Mr. Latta and others," but the chairman's chief concern was that the meeting not be interpreted as an endorsement of West and Johnson's actions. After all, everyone was there to quiet rumors, not incite them. Miner then sent the men of the reporting committee to draw up resolutions:

> *WHEREAS, Certain false statements have been put into circulation by newspaper correspondents and reporters that a considerable number of the people of Monroe have been engaged in the business of circulating counterfeit money; and that the sympathies of a large number of our people*

are with those who have heretofore been suspected of being engaged in that business, and,

WHEREAS, Recent acts of some members of our Village Board of Trustees, who have taken a conspicuous part in behalf of those suspected and arrested; and the act of the Monroe Brass Band, in serenading N.B. Latta on his return to our village, after having been released from jail upon the bond given by some members of our board of Trustees, have, in large measure, contributed to justify such suspicion; Therefore, it is, by the inhabitants of Monroe, in mass meeting assembled

RESOLVED, That it is not less the duty than the interest of the citizen to watch over the public morals and maintain the supremacy of the laws. To this end he should afford every possible aid to the detection and punishment of crime, and by his discreet conduct show to the vicious that only in repentance and reformation can he hope for sympathy or approval.

RESOLVED, That while we do not undertake to pronounce upon the guilt or innocence of any of the persons who have recently been arrested in our midst—leaving that to be determined by the civil courts—and while we disclaim all feelings of personal malice toward them, we heartily deprecate the attempts that have been made to forestall public sentiment in their favor, and give the appearance at least that men who rest under strong suspicion have the sympathy and confidence of the people of Monroe.

RESOLVED. That the conduct of the Monroe Brass Band in serenading a man lying under the charge of a great crime, merits our strongest reprehension; and that the fact of their being hired to do it relieves them of none of the responsibility, but should bring upon the party or parties who hired them, the swift condemnation due to one who has made himself the enemy of the public virtue, and the encourager of vice and crime.

RESOLVED. That while we respect those humane feelings that prompt one to relieve a fellow being in distress, and would not pronounce hastily upon the motives of men, yet we deem it particularly unfortunate that members of the Village Board should have so far identified themselves with parties…under suspicion, as to compromise the good name of Monroe, and that, under the circumstances, they ought to resign.

Fred West found the above so satisfactory that he motioned to have the resolutions printed in the *Chicago Tribune*, but nobody else thought that was a good idea. Readers may be interested to note that no village board member did resign—in fact, Dr. Johnson went on to serve the board again in 1873 and '79.

The chairman of the "Indignation Meeting," Samuel Elbert Miner, had good reason to take the position when Chenoweth and Churchill refused it. Miner was a probable relative of the Bonelatta's New York City distribution contact Joshua D. Miner, who organized the Ballard brothers' New York City affairs.

Reverend Samuel Elbert Miner (1815–1904) was from the Manassah Minor (1647–1728) branch of family patriarch Thomas Minor's Connecticut clan.[13] This same Manassah branch was represented in Steuben County, New York, from where Bonelatta Gang contact Joshua D. Miner learned the counterfeiting trade from his father[14] and very near where Latta bail man Dr. Johnson was elected to New York's House of Representatives in 1854.[15] In addition, both Joshua Miner and Dr. Johnson lived in Allegany County, New York, at around the same time: late 1840s–early 1850s.

Reverend Samuel Elbert Miner settled in Monroe, Wisconsin, in 1858, which was shortly after Napoleon Bonaparte Latta relocated his counterfeiting headquarters there.[16] Reverend Miner's relative Louisa Miner Young (1818–1888)[17] also moved to Monroe with her husband, Stephen Young (1813–?), and grown son Daniel during Latta's heyday.[18] Previously, the Youngs lived in Geauga, Ohio, but moved to the Illinois border with Wisconsin sometime around the eruption of the Mormon-lead Kirtland Safety Society banking scandal in 1837.[19]

Reverend Miner himself was not a New Yorker: he was from Halifax, Vermont, which lies near the Massachusetts border. Arabut Ludlow is believed to have been born around 1818 in the Burlington area of Vermont.

After a year of preaching in Monroe, Reverend Miner gave up the cloth to become a lumber merchant. Over the course of the Bonelatta Gang's heyday, Miner blossomed into one of the town's wealthy citizens. Was it coincidence that Reverend Samuel Elbert Miner and Louisa Miner Young's family came to Monroe and struck it rich during the town's dark period (1857–71) as a leading center for organized crime? The nature of nineteenth-century counterfeiting networks would suggest not. These crime networks were tight-knit extended family operations that grew as sons and cousins settled westward or daughters married into other counterfeiting families. In-group compliance was enforced via family ties and a culture of blood oaths. These families tended to engage in other crimes besides counterfeiting, particularly faith-based deceptions like divination, spirit-channeling or swindles stemming from purported commands from God.[20] Such scams found a rich field of victims in New England.

Reverend Samuel Elbert Miner was a man of great passion and self-righteousness. One of the first things that *The US Biographical Dictionary, Wisconsin Volume* (1877) tells us about the reverend is that his Pilgrim-derived Connecticut relatives were really honest: "not one of them ever having been accused of crime." The counterfeiting scandal involving Joshua D. Miner and the Bonelatta gang had broken in 1871; more Josh Miner scandals would break until his death in 1886.[21]

Prior to settling in Monroe, Reverend Miner was politically active as an abolitionist and studied at the Oneida Institution, a seminary that was shut down by the State of New York for its provocative activities: "Hundreds of young men were thus made to feel more intensely the curse of slavery, and became the life-long persistent enemies of that institution."[22]

"Abolitionism" enjoys uncritical praise in popular history. The truth is more complicated. Some abolitionists were violent radicals who relied on terrorism to achieve their aims and who trafficked low-cost labor to Northern employers.[23] Reverend Miner fit in comfortably with the 1840s–60s abolitionist crowd, raking in Wisconsin donations by railing against slavery in a non-slaveholding state, yet a state where bankers invested heavily in the slaveholding South.

In the 1840s, Reverend Miner was of the "congregational" persuasion, meaning his religious ideas were fashioned on the independent but sometimes extra-biblical teachings common in New England communities. One such community was the Bethlehem Settlement near Woodbury, Connecticut, where Justus Minor (1762–1850) was born before moving to Geauga, Ohio.[24] Justus was Louisa Miner Young's grandfather.[25] The inhabitants of the Bethlehem Settlement were famous for their religious extremism, which at times veered into antinomianism. As recorded by one of the Settlement's leading members, Dr. Joseph Bellamy:

> *In the fall of 1740, a little after Mr. Whitefield preacht through the country & in the Winter & Spring & Summer following, religion was again greatly revived & flourisht wonderfully.... The universal concern about religion in its height, many were seemingly converted, but there were false comfort & experiences among the rest which laid a foundation, (1) For False religion to rise & prevail (2) Many that were beat down, some fell into a melancholy, sour frame of spirit, bordering on despair, & others into carnal security; and the truly Godly seemed to be but a very few! And now very trying times follow, for (1) a number of the more elderly people being ambitious & having a grudge at each other are continually*

> *fomenting contention, strife and division about society affairs, (2) A number of the middle aged stand up for false religion & plead for the separatists, (3) A number of the younger sort set themselves up frolicking & serving the flesh—true piety & serious Godlines, are almost banished—this is a summary view of things from 1740 to 1750, & much so has it been in other places.*[26]

The Miner family was represented among practitioners of that religious radicalism and idealism which both graced and cursed New England. At the darker end of this spectrum we find men like Joshua D. Miner. But can we even be sure Joshua and Samuel Elbert are related? No extant census nor genealogical information on Joshua D. Miner remains. Sadly, it's not uncommon for notorious criminals like Joshua D. to "fall out" of the records of family histories or to find government-curated records denuded.

The good news is that newspaper-sourced details of Joshua's family life make it highly probable that his father was Marinus Willett Miner (1801–1871).[27] Marinus Willett had a son, "Charles M.," who was the right age to be Joshua Miner's less successful counterfeiter brother named "Charles M."[28] This Allegany County branch of the Miners descended from Marinus's dad, Absalom Miner (1771–1854) of New Haven, Connecticut, who had married into the notorious Rhode Island Gorton family.[29] Rhode Island has always been a hotbed of counterfeiting.[30]

Absalom Miner married Mary Gorton of Rhode Island in 1797, and at least two of their children moved to Allegany County, New York, alongside "Manassah"-branch cousins in neighboring Steuben County, where Joshua first ran afoul of the law. (Joshua was apprehended in the town of Wayland, about forty miles from where Marinus lived at Hume, Allegany County, New York.)[31] Given contemporary press reports that identify Joshua D. Miner's elders as intergenerational counterfeiters and the unfortunate situation in Rhode Island, Absalom's marriage suggests the typical pattern for intergenerational counterfeiting family networks. Absalom and two of his adult kids eventually moved to Friendship, New York.[32]

Given the probable family connections Samuel Ebert Miner had with Bone Latta's leading partner Josh Miner, it's hardly surprising that Samuel sought a place at the table heading off further investigations into Monroe's underworld.

No more counterfeiting investigations came to Monroe, despite the unforced errors of the *Sentinel* and the village board. This was probably less to do with the "Indignation Meeting" than prevailing political forces, which saw Napoleon Bonaparte Latta pardoned by President Rutherford B. Hayes, last of the Reconstruction presidents.[33] There was little will in Washington, D.C., to bring the gang behind Lincoln to justice.

Counterfeiting continued in Monroe after Bone Latta's arrest, but its disorganized nature was evidence that the head of the snake had been cut off. There was no upset to the town's ruling families: the agricultural fair, Universalist Church and bank chugged on as before. Things were getting far more interesting for Tom Ballard and the radical Republican Party of New York City, however.

4

LOUISVILLE, KENTUCKY

Napoleon Bonaparte Latta was the distribution kingpin for a counterfeiting network that predated his career. In the months before the Bonelatta Gang's breakup in Monroe, Operative Lonergan's superior at the Treasury, Colonel Hiram C. Whitley, had busted counterfeiters in locations that picked out the axis of this older criminal network: Kentucky, New York and Ohio.

The first dominoes fell with the capture of Dr. John P. McCartney. Dr. McCartney ran a family of counterfeiters who operated out of (1) Venice, Illinois (just across the Mississippi River from St. Louis, Missouri) and (2) Portland, Kentucky, which at that time was a village near Louisville on the Ohio River. Dr. McCartney was the type of man to whom Bone Latta would deliver "coney" (counterfeit currency):

> *For a while he* [Dr. McCartney] *went through this State* [Missouri] *delivering lectures on the best way of detecting counterfeit money, and making from fifty to one hundred dollars a night by so doing, together with disposing of a great quantity of the "queer"* [counterfeit currency] *at good profit.*[1]

McCartney's mistake had been returning to Louisville to establish a new printing base: he'd offered to pay far too much in rent for a shack, which made the prospective landlord nervous. In the preceding fifteen years, Louisville had seen more than its fair share of counterfeiting crime,

Mississippi and Ohio Riverways were crucial for counterfeiting networks. McCartney's bases are marked with stars. In 1782, Bertha Palmer's great-grandfather Jean Antoine Honoré first opened these waterways for traffic.

and the rattled landlord went straight to the sheriff, who went straight to Colonel Whitley.

McCartney's numerous contacts included German counterfeiter Fred Biebusch, who was already being tried thanks to Whitley.[2] At the same time McCartney was apprehended, agents also picked up Indiana counterfeiter Charley Johnson of the notorious Johnson crime family.

These arrests shocked the criminal underworld. The day after McCartney's arrest, an important witness named Bill Gurney was caught trying to break out of his jail cell with a "hammer, saws and sledges."[3] Gurney was an asset to Colonel Whitley's work cutting out the New York heart of the Bonelattas. Subsequent arrests spread into Indiana, Wisconsin and Ohio.[4] America's native counterfeiting dynasties were being systematically put out of business.

Louisville, Kentucky, stands out as odd as a location for this criminal axis: New England had been a hotbed of global counterfeiting since colonial times. Ohio, as gateway to lawless borderlands, was a natural hangout for miscreants. But Louisville had been settled and policed a for a long time by the mid-1800s. Why Louisville?

The answer to that question starts in Cincinnati, Ohio, in 1853. Desperate policemen from Louisville asked their peers in Cincinnati for help busting a politically connected counterfeiting ring that spanned their two states. Kentucky policemen knew they couldn't investigate this ring without reprisals from their local political patrons.[5]

The Kentucky-Ohio ring included educated men, particularly medical doctors,[6] who used Covington, Kentucky, on the Ohio River as distribution channel. The ring printed fake bills in Cincinnati at the premises of an esteemed engraving company: Rawdon, Wright, Hatch, and Edson (RWH&E). This company was based in New York City but operated satellite offices in New Orleans, Boston and Philadelphia in addition to their Ohio branch. A gold standard firm, RWH&E was the first engraver to receive a government contract for manufacturing U.S. postage stamps.[7] Allegedly, it was one rogue RWH&E employee who used his spare time to counterfeit Ohio State Stock Bank notes, which the firm also produced legitimately.

Why medical doctors in a counterfeiting ring? One of the curious aspects of mid-nineteenth-century counterfeiting was its synergy with the medical community. Gangs often counted doctors—or at least men who passed themselves off as doctors—among their members. It's possible that this profession was a useful cover because no one would second guess why doctors had the money or cause to travel regularly.

However, it would be a mistake to overlook the fact that nineteenth-century doctors who had legal, political or social trouble in more civilized areas sometimes ran to the Midwest, where medical men were scarce and patients were desperate. Settlers often went to quacks for cures; for example, the "homeopathic physician" trade was well represented in Monroe, Wisconsin. Arabut Ludlow's banking partner's daughter Dr. Helen Bingham was a homeopathic doctor. Like counterfeiting, quack medicine was a racket for cons with capital and would therefore have attracted people of similar ethics.

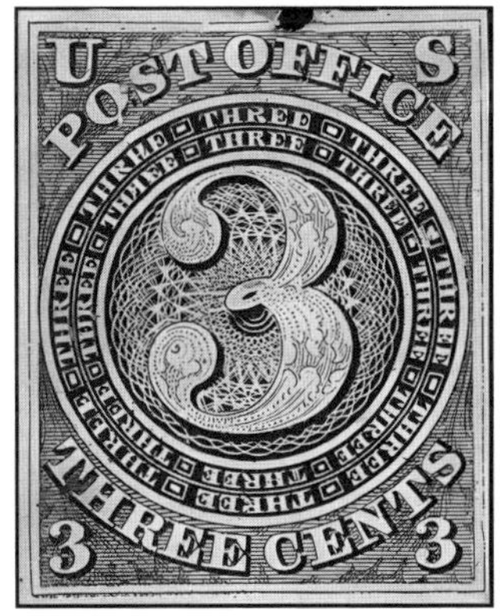

United States three-cent stamp engraved by Rawdon, Wright, Hatch and Edson. *Private collection.*

Unfortunately for the Kentucky-Ohio gang, the Cincinnati detectives were both honest and dedicated.[8] In 1853, they began to systematically round up the gang. The Kentucky-Ohio dominoes fell from shover, to distribution men, to finally the engraver at RWH&E, Ransel Lamb. However, just like with Detective Lonergan in Monroe, the politically connected top layer of the gang was never prosecuted,[9] although we know they existed because of the Louisville police's initial pleas.

After RWH&E's involvement with counterfeiting was revealed, the company deemphasized its Cincinnati office.[10] The firm's executives retreated to New York City and in 1858 reestablished their company as the American Bank Note Company.[11] As RWH&E was the Treasury's sole engraving contractor, Tom Ballard could have learned about U.S. Treasury notes only from this firm.

RWH&E's treasurer Neziah Wright,[12] a New England native, participated in the firm's reorganization in New York. New England "backwater" states along the border with Canada had been home to counterfeiting clans since the Revolutionary War. The British used counterfeiting in economic warfare against the rebelling Americans. Some of these counterfeiters found sanctuary in Canada, where they continued their operations when the fighting was over. This is the genesis of the famed criminal highway from Canada "Cogniac Street" and the slang term for counterfeiters "koniackers."[13]

The New England criminal clans who remained stateside spread West as public tolerance for counterfeiting waned after the 1830s. Yet in 1850s New York City, Neziah Wright and other company executives lost no time hiring employees as ethical as Ransel Lamb. It wasn't long before Tom Ballard was abusing Treasury and other national bank plates in exactly the same way Lamb had done back in Cincinnati.

The dissolution of the Kentucky-Ohio gang opened up opportunities for other criminals. In the months that RWH&E was reinventing itself, life took an exciting turn for a young jailbird in Ohio named Joshua D. Miner, whose family we met in the previous chapter.

Joshua Miner belonged to a family of intergenerational counterfeiters, and young Josh had fled New York to Ohio in 1854 in order to escape parenting an illegitimate daughter.[14] While there, he "shoved" fake $5 bills and was caught, convicted and entered the Ohio Penitentiary on June 26, 1855. Miner then escaped jail one month into his sentence; he was recaptured almost three years later in February 1858 and exactly one month after that he was pardoned for everything by Ohio's Radical Republican Governor Salmon Portland Chase.

Chase's pardon documentation shows that young Miner had extraordinary political cheerleaders by 1858. When reading the transcript that follows, bear in mind that on Miner's release he would immediately scurry up to New York City and begin counterfeiting on an industrial scale using probable American Bank Note Company employee Tom Ballard. As dictated by Governor Chase:

> *Joshua Miner, for having in possession with intent to sell counterfeit Bank Bills, was sentenced at the May term 1955, by the Court of Common Pleas of Cuyahoga County, to imprisonment in the Penitentiary for three years.*
>
> *The original application for pardon in this case was made some months since. Having ascertained that the convict had escaped form the Penitentiary and was then at large, declined to consider the application or look at any papers connected with it until he should have surrendered him self to custody; and advised the parties applying, that upon such surrender the case must rest wholly on the merits as they should then appear independently of such surrender.*
>
> *Having been advised this day by the Warden of the Penitentiary that the convict has surrendered himself and is now in actual custody, I have examined the papers and find that the officer who arrested Miner upon the charge of which he was convicted now entertains strong doubts of his guilt, which doubts are shared by six of the jurors who rendered the verdict of guilty; that these doubts arise upon facts developed since the trial; the Judge who tried the case states that the evidence on the trial was such that the Jury might have acquitted as well as convicted him; and that the Police Judge, the City Marshall* [sic], *The Chief and members of Police of the city of Cleveland, all concur in thinking the original conviction wrong. It is already shown that the prisoner sustained a good character before his conviction and since his escape, now nearly three years since, has so conducted himself as to gain the confidence and respect of the community in which he lives, he as married respectably and is engaged in honest business. It is further stated by the former and present Prosecuting Attorney that his testimony is required in important investigations and cannot be given while he is under the disability of conviction*[.] *Under these circumstances his pardon is recommended by Magistrates and officers already referred to: by all the Jurors who have been seen except two; buy the Common Pleas and Probate Judges; by many members of the bar, and by the Senator and Representatives from the County. Two jurors remonstrate but only on the grounds that they*

> *think the original conviction correct and that the case is not a proper one for Executive interposition. This remonstrance cannot in justice be permitted to overthrow the very strong case made for the prisoner, who is therefore pardoned.*
> *March 5, 1858*[15]

Miner was a shover, a low-level gang member, when convicted in 1855. During his nearly three years on the lam, he married, became a carpenter, learned valuable information regarding an "important" ongoing criminal investigation and captured the hearts of Cleveland's entire police force and legislative representatives.

Salmon Portland Chase is famous to history as Abraham Lincoln's Treasury secretary and father of the "greenback" national currency. This parentage is somewhat misplaced, but Chase did arrange to have his face portrayed on the first greenback bills as a way of boosting his political image:

> *I went to work and made "greenbacks" and a good many of them. I had some handsome pictures put on them; and as I like to be among the people, and was kept too close to visit them in any other way, and as the engravers thought me rather good looking, I told them they might put me on the end of the one-dollar bills.*[16]

Top: U.S. Treasury note featuring Chase's portrait. Engraved by the National Banknote Company, an 1859 spinoff from the American Banknote Company, which would remerge in 1879. *American Numismatic Association.*

Bottom: Reverse of the Chase portrait note. *American Numismatic Association.*

Chase didn't make his name in finance. He gained fame as a lawyer in Cincinnati who championed the estate of Israel Ludlow and abolitionism, in that order.

Chase's early career in Cincinnati focused heavily on the affairs of his then-wife's family estate.[17] Chase married his third wife, Sarah Bella Dunlop Ludlow, in 1846 and was soon employed sorting out the legal entanglements of her land-rich grandfather Israel Ludlow. Ludlow was an early surveyor of Ohio who focused on the lands that made up Cincinnati. His family had settled in New Jersey before the Revolutionary War and would have experienced Governor William Livingston's sweeping wartime powers.

When Chase wasn't busy unpicking land disputes for his in-laws, he dedicated himself to protecting "fugitive slaves" and that strange class of free men who made money either returning slaves to their owners or trafficking them to new employers in the North. Chase eschewed calling himself an "abolitionist" because that term had violent connotations and was politically unsaleable. Instead, Chase chose to call himself "antislavery" because his primary political goal was to undermine the power of Southern slaveholders. In the words of biographer Walter Stahr:

> *The best way to achieve change, he* [Chase] *believed, was through politics, by building a broad antislavery political party. He hoped and expected that, once an antislavery party took control of the national government, the states would change their own laws and that slavery would end, though he was vague about how this would occur. But the first task was to wrest control of the federal government from the Southern slave owners.*[18]

Chase's goal was to reorganize how political power was shared among the United States' elite; making enslaved labor available as "free" labor was a close second. The subtle distinction between *abolitionist* and *antislavery* dissolves apparent contradictions between Chase's, and Chase champions like William H. Seward's, attitudes toward different laboring groups. We met Seward in chapter 1 with regard to his support for Allan Pinkerton and in chapter 2 with regard to Latta serenader Dr. Lucien B. Johnson.

From his earliest days as an antislavery advocate, Chase coordinated with William H. Seward, scion of the prominent New York political family.[19] Since before the Revolution, New York politics had been dominated by a network of landowning patrician families such as the Livingstons and their in-laws the van Rensselaers. William Henry Seward acted as a political advocate for these families.[20]

The Livingstons were consummate politicians with a monarchist agenda.[21] This family's New World goal was to re-create the feudal system they enjoyed back in Scotland under the Stuarts. To that end, they supported the British monarchy but *not* Parliament. They only sold out the British king once the prospect of their absolute power in the New Jersey colony became a possibility—circa 1775.

The Livingstons distrusted democratic institutions. Between their mercenary armies and newspaper investments, the family intimidated and manipulated early New England electorates, whom they treated like serfs.[22] The Livingstons' serfs were not enslaved Black laborers or American Indians but the humble white settlers who toiled to make New England farmland valuable.

While the Livingstons and their peers believed themselves to be aristocrats, they operated like an organized crime syndicate. Besides controlling prostitution[23] and piracy,[24] these patrician families made their fortunes through seizing settlers' farmland.[25] Sometimes these settlers had rented land from American Indian landlords like the Wappinger Tribe,[26] or sometimes they purchased it. Once the difficult work of improvement had been done, the patrician families would then lay claim to the land and use their henchmen in colonial government to make these seizures retroactively legal.

The patrician families employed private armies to terrorize any farmers who resisted. Dispossessed farmers were then forced to rent back their land at unfavorable rates. As time progressed, these "tenant farmers" were compelled by law to work without pay, just like serfs or slaves. When they revolted, their leaders were sentenced according to British law regarding slave revolts: to be hanged, drawn and quartered. The most famous revolt leader to receive this sentence was William Prendergast, leader of the 1766 Dutchess County, New York uprising.[27]

Early in his career as governor of New York, William H. Seward had to deal with one of these tenant revolts. He ignored the demands of the tenants and protected the forced-labor privileges of the van Rensselaer family. Yet history remembers Seward as an "abolitionist." Could it be that Seward believed in abolition for Black people, not White? Or were his motives more complicated?

One answer is provided by the history of Governor William Livingston in New Jersey (1723–1790). Governor Livingston enjoyed almost absolute power during the course of the Revolution. Livingston punished smugglers severely, but ignored his own relatives' illegal trade with Great Britain. His draconian attempts to rout out traitors never reached the Loyalists in his own family.[28] Livingston's reign of terror and corruption came to an end only when pro-democracy New Jersey state legislators stood up to him. His dreams of federal kingship were undermined when Southern delegates at the Constitutional Convention organized against him.[29] Consequently, Livingston joined his radical Quaker friends promoting abolitionism while quietly acquiring more slaves himself!

New England's "aristocracy" didn't like having their power checked. Could it be that New England abolitionism was simply a tool through which the privileged could seize more power?

From his earliest days as an "antislavery activist," Chase coordinated his efforts with William H. Seward via New York financier Lewis Tappan.[30] The trio's goal was to break Southern power by forming an "antislavery" party out of disaffected Whigs and Democrats. A secondary goal was to prevent slave owners from repatriating slaves who fled to work in the North.

Former slaves were a vulnerable, and therefor exploitable, labor pool. Northern industrialists relied on such displaced labor, though they usually employed European immigrants fleeing starvation or political persecution. Once relocated to America's urban centers, these immigrants were paid poorly, crammed into unhealthy tenements, employed in dangerous factories and forced to vote according to gangsters' contracts with urban elites. Seward had partnered with one of these gangsters, Thurlow Weed, a railroad investor and Whig political boss in Albany, New York.

Thurlow Weed was a political fixer for railroad magnate Erastus Corning, who controlled one of two rail lines connecting Chicago with New York City. Corning was a Democrat but the type with whom Whigs Weed and Seward did successful railway business.[31]

If the plight of New England's tenant farmers wasn't enough to tug antislavery heartstrings, surely the plight of urban immigrants would be? But here too Chase and Seward were on the side of privilege.[32] In the 1840s, American-born freemen organized to protect their health, democratic government and livelihoods from industrialists who paid low wages, operated unsafe workplaces and handed cities to organized crime via mass immigration. These freemen called themselves the "Know Nothings" because they used secrecy in the face of political persecution. Chase and Seward were anti–Know Nothing from the first because cheap immigrant labor was important to the North's ruling class. Was oppressing labor in the North a "Christian" stance, while oppressing labor in the South "evil"?

Albany, New York's Whig political boss and railroad investor Thurlow Weed. *Library of Congress.*

Chase was active in Universalist circles on the subject of antislavery,[33] and I remind readers that Universalism was the religion of Monroe, Wisconsin's elite. Bone Latta's bail provider, Dr. Johnson, was a legislative colleague of New York State representative Lucius S. May, who got himself burned in effigy for going back on promises to his Know Nothing constituents and voting for William Seward in 1854.

The last inch of Chase's antislavery mask slips away when one considers his motivation for opposing the Kansas-Nebraska Act of 1854. Senator Stephen Douglas's reason for bringing the act was railway development. In order to get the act passed, he had to make Midwestern railway opportunities open to Southern investors.[34] This would dilute antislavery control of Northern transportation lines around Chicago, perhaps even destroy such control, because the South was competitive in railway building. From historian William G. Thomas of the University of Nebraska, Lincoln:

> *By 1860 the South was the third leading railroad nation in the world, trailing only the northern United States and the United Kingdom in total miles constructed. It contained 33 percent of the nation's railroad mileage and 40 percent of its population, and southern states were aggressively promoting railroad development throughout the 1850s.*[35]

Southern railway developers enjoyed an advantage because they owned or rented slaves, who were cheaper labor for dangerous track-construction work. This was bad for railway developers like Erastus Corning or Thurlow Weed, who had to pay *not quite as low* wages based on the "free" market of desperate immigrants in the North. Thurlow Weed's covetous attitude toward Southern slave labor probably explains his investment in the Underground Railway, which brought even cheaper labor to Northern railway developers.[36]

The dark underbelly of the Underground Railroad is that it was a trafficking network for bringing vulnerable labor northward on an industrial scale. This trafficking undermined Northern workers' attempts to win fair wages and safe working conditions. In the words of labor historian Edna Bonacich:

> *Both slaves and free blacks are found to have been lower-priced sources of labor than whites, to whom they therefore posed a threat of displacement. Slavery was a system which gave southern capitalists total control of a cheap labor force, permitting extensive displacement. It also put the South*

> *in conflict with northern capital, because the latter depended on higher-priced (white) labor. Abolition threatened to increase competition between black and white labor, spreading the problem to all regions and segments of the economy.*[37]

A tragic example of this vulnerability is none other than Harriet Tubman. Once "free" in the North, Tubman was financially dependent on William H. Seward's family.[38] Tubman worked hard in furtherance of Seward's antislavery agenda, both as a lobbyist and as a military fighter.[39]

The type of men Chase defended in Ohio, like Underground Railroad trafficker John van Zandt, were the forerunners of our modern trafficking "snakeheads" or "coyotes." Often they were Quakers (for example shoe-factory owner Thomas Garrett)[40] or freed Blacks themselves.[41] They weren't all idealists:

> *However, more for-profit activity took place in the migration brokerage of escaped slaves than popular narratives of the underground generally reveal. Alongside and often working with abolitionist activists, many people played for-profit roles in the Underground Railroad, charging slaves and activists for passage aboard ships or other forms of collaboration.*[42]

These charges were paid by "stockholders"[43] in the Underground Railroad—a term the activists actually used for their wealthy Northern financiers like Weed and Seward.

While some traffickers may have been ethically motivated, others trafficked for money and were as ready to take payments to return slaves to owners as to free them. Chase's own papers document this moral ambiguity: on March 4, 1855 Chase records one trafficker, attorney John L. Pendery, who chose a $10 payment to return escaped slave Rosetta Armstead, rather than a $5 payment to release her northward.[44] This same Pendery asked Chase's political associate William Martin Dickson for a $10 loan. Dickson then *gave* Pendery $10 but didn't want anything back in return considering Pendery's ignoble way of making money. The relationship between "antislavery activists" and "kidnappers" for the "Slave Power" was sometimes complicated.

Allan Pinkerton is another example of such complication. Pinkerton used his connections with the railroads around Chicago to traffic enslaved people northward to new employers. He did this alongside terrorist John Brown and with the blessing of the Chicago Judiciary Convention and

Allan and Joan Pinkerton. Their Chicago home was "bursting at the seams" with Underground Railway "runaways" whom Allan systematically trafficked northward (See James Mackay, *Allen Pinkerton: The First Private Eye* [John Wiley and Sons, 1997], 83–85). *Library of Congress.*

Michigan Central Railroad.[45] As Pinkerton's biographer James D. Horan described him:

> *While Pinkerton's right hand caught lawbreakers, his left hand broke the law. But his conscience was, of course, clear as that of any Quaker patriot out on the long Underground route.*[46]

A holistic view of the Underground Railroad places it in the context of existing smuggling networks, including the counterfeiting networks that Chase's pardon-recipient Joshua D. Miner helped put to Lincoln's service during the Civil War. Seward's—or his political backers'—probable employment of the pro-abolition Bonelatta network is doubly interesting in light of Seward's support for the Underground Railroad.[47]

The most important way Chase helped the "antislavery party" take control of the national government was through wartime financial measures: the National Currency and National Banking Acts (1863). The financial know-how for this maneuver came from William H. Seward's political camp.

5

"JOT" MINER IN NEW YORK CITY

On October 26, 1871, when Bone Latta nervously awaited his counterfeiting trial in La Crosse, Wisconsin, Colonel Hiram C. Whitley of the Secret Service's New York City office was unpicking the eastern branch of Latta's ring. Threads began unraveling from Chicago, where a series of arrests led to Joshua D. "Jot" Miner. By early November, Whitley had arrested Miner, who was indicted in New York City on seventeen counts of counterfeiting and faced 255 years in prison.[1]

By the late 1860s Jot Miner had come a long way from where we first met him in Cincinnati.[2] He was now a consummate mid-nineteenth-century New York City politician: "good-looking and gentlemanly," probably near forty, with muttonchop whiskers and the air of a banker.[3] A Radical Republican, Miner liked to flaunt his expensive mare Lady Allen next to Commodore Vanderbilt's horses during the Sleighing Carnival in Central Park, which was a nineteenth-century high-society "cruising" event.[4]

This sort of luxury was expensive, and Miner met those costs through a mixture of business and politics. From 1866 on, Miner always served New York City's nineteenth district through typical "boodle"-type appointments. His legitimate business—if you can call it that—was street repair contracting for the city, and he employed over one hundred men in this capacity.[5]

As one might expect, Joshua Miner abused his office: in March 1869, fully two years prior to what is believed to be the beginning of the "Whiskey Ring" operating around President Grant's cabinet, Josh Miner and Thomas O'Callaghan (tax collector for NYC's ninth district) were indicted for illegally removing one hundred barrels of whiskey from a distillery on Fifty-Fourth Street.[6]

Things first came crashing down for Miner in June 1871 for reasons removed from money. His wife, Loretta, the lady he'd married prior to his meteoric rise in Cincinnati, had died.[7] Whether her loss made him sloppy or he lost underworld protection from her family is hard to discern. What we know is that the winter of 1871 brought the first in a series of court cases he would spend the next five years fighting: counterfeiting charges stemming from the Ballard brothers' bust outside of Monroe, Wisconsin.

Miner's counterfeiting indictment came on November 6, and he was released on bail of $30,000 two weeks later, at which time Colonel Whitley said that he'd been offered a $200,000 bribe to abandon the prosecution.[8] Secret Service agents believed they were unwinding not just a local New York gang but the most "troublesome and skillful" gang of counterfeiters in the country.[9]

Law enforcement had their work cut out for them. Miner was a millionaire and immediately retained very capable lawyers who began a strategy of delaying the trial and attacking the credibility of Secret Service agents.[10] Unfortunately, this was easy to do because the Secret Service had been staffed by criminals eager to take revenge on their competitors. Time and time again over the course of Miner's trial we see that his lawyers know all the skeletons in the Service's closet—for example, this line of questioning for Operative Drummond:

> *The witness* [Drummond] *was cross-examined at great length. He admitted that he had been once arrested for being in a drunken crowd in New York, and that, on another occasion, while drunk, as he believed, he had fallen through a shoemaker's window in Bangor, Me; he was arrested for that and taken to the station; he paid $250, and was discharged in the morning.*[11]

Portrait of Secret Service head Colonel Hiram C. Whitley. Whitley served under the gambling-friendly Major General Benjamin Franklin Butler in New Orleans. *Wikipedia.*

Lawyers for the state were equally determined. The onslaught began with Chicago counterfeiter Henry C. Cole's testimony. Cole explained how he had agreed to buy counterfeit printing plates and money from Miner as part of a plan devised by Colonel Hiram C. Whitley.

We met Colonel Whitley before during Agent Lonergan's June testimony in Janesville, Wisconsin.

Lonergan had refused a leniency deal in exchange for Latta's evidence about Eastern counterfeiters whom Whitley was investigating.

Colonel Whitley was chief of the Secret Service Department of the United States Treasury and a man very conscious of his power. This is how the colonel described himself during Miner's trial, which began on December 12, 1871:

> *I have branch offices in all large cities; I have a branch office in New York, at No. 52 Bleecker street; we do more business in other cities; I was appointed Chief of the Secret Service Department, I think, on the 12th of May, 1869; in 1867 I was in the Revenue Service, in a position of the same nature; I am familiar with counterfeit money.*[12]

(The funding for Colonel Whitley's operations was controlled by George Ellis Baker, a political crony of William H. Seward who, as Lincoln's secretary of state, had Baker appointed "disbursing clerk and administrator" for the Secret Service Fund.[13] Baker's son George Fisher Baker is the subject of chapter 6.)

Whitley personifies the staffing problems that plagued the Service: it was often difficult to distinguish agents from their quarry.[14] One issue that Miner's defense brought up was that of the "Radcliffe Diamonds." Colonel Whitley had received a package of smuggled diamonds "from a broker downtown [in New York City]" worth about $230. The colonel accepted these jewels and divided them up among his men. He defended his actions by saying "there was never any criminal charge brought against me in relation to those diamonds."[15] Prior to joining the Revenue Service, Whitley was a pawnbroker in Boston and had his license revoked in consequence of a fraud charge involving a watch.

By his own admission, Colonel Whitley had led an interesting life. Before the pawn business, he was a fraud detective in New Orleans for the disgraced Union General Benjamin Butler, himself a Radical Republican and what we would now call a civil rights firebrand. Whitley joined Butler, having worked in Kansas assisting in the capture of fugitive slaves—quite the sort of man with whom lawyer Salmon P. Chase was used to dealing.[16] The path to Reconstruction law enforcement could be convoluted.

Miner's lawyers knew that Whitley's relationship with Miner was cordial, as the colonel explained:

> *On the 25th of August, 1870, I had Bill Gurney under arrest in my office; he is a notorious counterfeiter; I went with Gurney in a carriage to see Mr.*

> *Miner. . . .As we got up near the stable we saw Miner come up; he said to Gurney, "How are you, Old Stick in the Mud?" Gurney introduced me to Miner; Gurney told Miner he was in trouble; Miner said he could do nothing for him; I took Miner aside and told him I had satisfactory information that he had those $20 plates, that Gurney had been arrested with a large number of the bills on him; Miner denied that he had the plates, but I insisted that he had; finally he said, "I guarantee that you shall have those $20 plates"; he said he did not want his name mixed up in the papers with Gurney, as he supposed there would be a big long article about it in the papers; I said I would not put his name in the papers with Gurney; Miner appointed a meeting with me in the lower part of the Astor House; I went there at the appointed time; this was a few days after he had told me he would surrender the plates; I met Miner there; he said the matter was all right; that I should have these plates in a few days; he told me to come to his house. . . .*
>
> *Some ten or fifteen days after I went to Mr. Miner's house; Miner came to the door and took me in; I talked to him for a considerable time about counterfeiting business; he said he was not quite ready to give up the plates, as he had to go to the races; I told him I hoped he would give up this counterfeiting business, as it only injured the poor and not the government; he rose his hands and said, "I give you may word I will have nothing more to do with counterfeiting business, so help me God"; I told him that Gurney was a bad man, and that I did not want to use him as a witness against him; that Gurney had offered to me to buy counterfeiting money of him, Miner; Miner said, "Suppose I took Gurney into my buggy, with a fast horse and drive out on the road to see my man, what could you do?"*[17]

As one might expect, Whitley didn't talk Miner out of the counterfeiting business. Whitley ended up using Cole, a fellow engraver with "eyes deeply sunken, and of a cadaverous appearance,"[18] to engineer a trap for Miner. Cole would trick Miner into accepting counterfeiting plates and $1,500 in marked real money[19] in exchange for Cole's freedom.

The maneuver took place at seven o'clock on the night of October 25, 1871. Whitley sent two men to "pipe" (secretly follow) Cole and warned them that Miner never made a hand-off without a third man ready, watching from the background. Cole started out from the corner of Fifty-Ninth Street and Ninth Avenue at 6:30 p.m.[20] Operative Applegate, one of the shadows, was not to arrest Miner unless Cole successfully made the exchange, which he would signal by dropping his hat. Applegate described Whitley's plan:

Whitley told me to go up to Fifty-ninth street to meet Cole, search him and then follow him up to connect with Miner, to see them "make a deal" for a set of plates; this was at five o'clock in the evening; before that Colonel Whitley took $1,500; it was marked and given to Cole in a lager beer saloon in the Bowery....Cole then walked up toward Sixty-seventh street....I saw Cole with Miner; I was standing a little below on the sidewalk....I remained behind a dirt pile until I saw Cole come up to Miner, and as they came together Kennoch seized Miner, and as he was seized by the collar Miner threw the package of plates toward me....I kept my eye on the package, expecting that if any one came up I should arrest him; I expected that some one connected with Miner might come up to aid him and if he did I would arrest him; Kennoch and Miner were squabbling, and I helped Kennoch to put irons on Miner.[21]

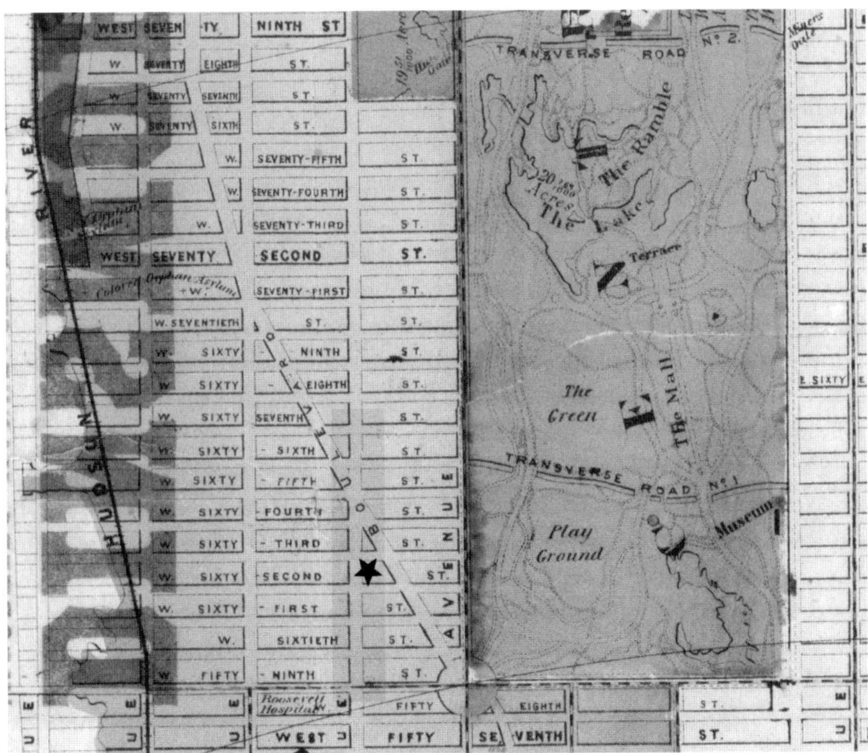

An 1871 NYC map showing where Operative Applegate says Miner was apprehended on Sixty-Second Street (starred), probably outside Lady Allen's stable. Shaded rectangle marks area of chase. *Library of Congress.*

It was during this "squabble" that the marked $1,500 Whitley had given to Cole exploded over said "dirt pile"—sweepings from Miner's stable at Broadway and Sixty-Seventh Streets.[22] Applegate testified that as Kennoch and Miner wrestled in the dirt, a northeasterly wind blew the real money all over and that a third operative was tasked with chasing the bills down and cataloguing them. This caused peals of laughter in the courtroom. Applegate:

> *I sent Kennoch after Cole; he got him; Miner, Cole, Kennoch and myself got into the carriage and drove down to the office in Bleecker street; Kennoch opened the package.... Inside was a green cloth and inside that were the plates.... I did not see the arrest of the man who gave the plates to Miner; this man gave his name as Evey, but I believe his real name is Thomas Ballard.*[23]

At the time of Ballard's arrest, Colonel Whitley had never seen him before and didn't know where he operated: this makes Ballard unique among the counterfeiters. Ballard produced exquisite forgeries of national bank and Treasury bills.[24] Described as a "genius" by law enforcement biographer John Dye,[25] Tom Ballard knew all the Treasury's (and the American Bank Note Company's) manufacturing secrets.[26] The son of English immigrants, he achieved this expertise by twenty years old and was described as five foot nine, genteel and "with a face that is handsome almost to a captivating point."[27] The agents had bagged their "third man," but he was a bigger fish than they understood at the time. Both Miner and Ballard were under arrest in Whitley's Bleecker Street office by 8:30 p.m. and were held in jail until the following day.[28]

The arrest of Tom Ballard's brother John near Gratiot, Wisconsin, on July 2, 1871, had done little to slow down Tom's New York City counterfeiting career. On the night Colonel Whitley caught Tom, he was selling a $10 plate for printing counterfeit on the National Bank of Poughkeepsie and a $2 plate from the Ninth National Bank of New York City.[29]

"What is this for?" Tom Ballard asked as the agents grabbed him.

"You have robbed a friend of mine," Operative Drummond answered.

Ballard scanned the group of men and saw Miner's face. "This cannot be for robbery," he countered. Of course, Tom was right.[30]

When Ballard reached Whitley's office, he wisely stopped talking. After a night in jail, however, he gave up his "laboratory," which consisted of rooms in a tenement house at 256 Rivington Street. When agents raided the

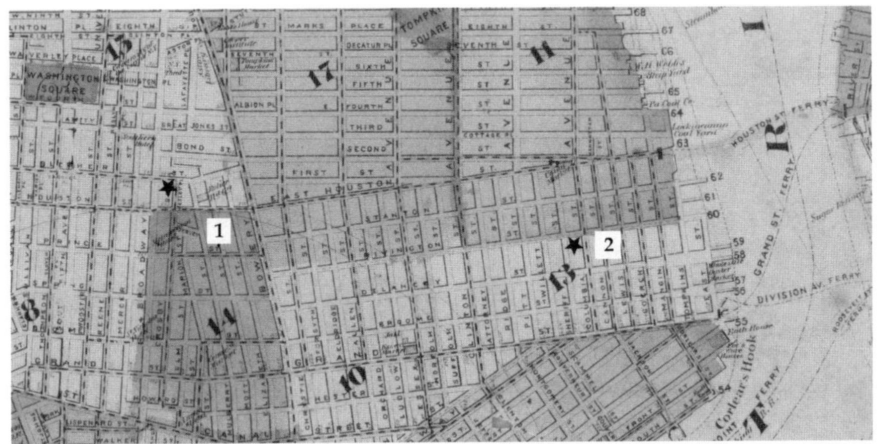

An 1871 NYC map showing (1) the Secret Service's New York Office and (2) the location of Tom Watson's 256 Rivington Street tenement-factory. *Library of Congress.*

lab, they found that John Ballard, Tom's brother and one of the "Watson brothers" in Monroe, had lived there too.

At 256 Rivington, agents found two presses, one ruling machine (cutter for the bills), two sets of engravers' tools and—most fascinating of all—a quantity of the new fiber paper that the Treasury used to prevent counterfeiting. This thick paper was shot through with visible dark fibers called jute, and the process for making it was secret. "Ballard is the only man outside the government employ who understands making fibre paper," proclaimed the *New York Daily Herald*, and this was probably true.[31] Colonel Whitley testified that the Treasury Secretary George S. Boutwell wanted Tom Ballard in particular (or wanted to make a show of wanting him), and approved a $5,000 award for Ballard's arrest, five times the amount Whitley was originally prepared to reward.[32]

Besides about $3,500 in counterfeit bills, the agents found inks, colors and a bunch of $1,000 Treasury notes "of new United States issue." A consequent raid on the home of Lewellyn Williams at 438 West Fifty-Fourth Street uncovered more counterfeiting paraphernalia and of course fake bills. (The press described all these counterfeiters as "English.") Williams and Ballard were working together using the fiber paper. Tom Ballard and Miner were confined to the Ludlow Street Jail on $25,000 bail each, but Ballard, the star witness, escaped before Miner's trial.[33] Counterfeiters escaped jail lamentably often during the Grant administration.[34] Therefore, it was the testimony from Tom's brother John Ballard that was used against Miner.[35]

Chicago newspapers carried little about the Joshua D. Miner trial *except* an excerpt from John Ballard's testimony, which the *Tribune*'s editors must have felt had special meaning to local readers:

> *I am 32 years old, and a printer by trade. Up to last month I was engaged off and on in manufacturing counterfeit money. The place where I have carried on operations principally is 256 Rivington Street* [since 1868], *where I had full control using two printing presses. There is a process of driving up the letters that give the name of the bank so that they may be filed down, and new names engraved and printed from them as counterfeits on other banks. The twenty dollar plate which is here has been filled down in this way at least twenty-eight times. Farmers' and Mechanics' Bank of Poughkeepsie, being the last counterfeit. I have been engaged over three years at 235 Rivington street, at this kind of printing, generally turning out about $10,000 a month.*
>
> *Cross-examined:* [John Ballard continues] [I] *Was arrested once in Buffalo for manufacturing silver Mexican shillings, tried, convicted and sentenced to five years and four months' imprisonment in the Auburn State Prison. Four years and two months of this time I served, when I was pardoned by the Governor. The petition for pardon was made by Colonel Whitley. After I had been out of prison two years I began to counterfeit again. The first I did at it after I was released was to counterfeit fifty-cent currency notes, in Lewis Street.... I moved to 250 Rivington Street, where I went into the business wholesale. Then I went out to Wisconsin and hired a farm, from there I went to jail. I was implicated in counterfeiting out there, but was not guilty. I am still under arrest, however, waiting for my trial. Colonel Whitley brought me here on a writ of habeas corpus to take part as witness in this case.*[36]

John Ballard had been brought from jail to make this testimony,[37] but none of the New York papers carried the information regarding John Ballard's pardon from the governor of New York or why Whitley had an interest in securing it. As Miner's trial progressed, things became increasingly unflattering for the Treasury Department. Miner, John Ballard's post-pardon employer, was identified as the originator of bogus $100 compound interest notes produced in 1864, of which $750,000 was put in circulation.[38] Much of the equipment Whitley's men seized from Ballard was specifically designed to counterfeit Treasury notes. What they found must have made Treasury officials nauseated:

> *One $1,000 plate, in an unfinished state; one $20 greenback, fully finished, back and front; one $10 national bank (Poughkeepsie Bank), on steel; one do*[llar], *not finished, the back only being engraved; one $2 national bank, on steel, fully completed.*
>
> *Ten transfer rolls (hardened steel) for reproducing duplicates of all the above, except the $1000 plate.*
>
> *Ten full sets, original vel pieces* [hardened steel] *for making transfer rolls.*
>
> *One transfer press costing $10,700, of a kind rarely found outside of the Treasury Department or bank note companies.*
>
> *One transfer press, smaller pattern, costing $1,200…*
>
> *A full set of Treasury seals for stamping the red seal impressions on the notes.*
>
> *About one hundred and fifty pounds of the celebrated "fibre" paper and the entire apparatus required to make the same.*[39]

The implications of this haul were disastrous for the Treasury itself, which at best showed incompetence and at worst suggested official complicity with Miner, Ballard and Williams.

Jurors then learned that that Abram C. Beatty, the Treasury agent who received the first counterfeiting plates from Miner back in 1870 when Whitley allegedly tried to talk Miner out of a life of crime,[40] was actually now an employee of Miner. Beatty had been let go of from the Service the previous November when it came to light that he used his Treasury position to blackmail shopkeepers. Further investigation showed that in 1865 Beatty had murdered his rival in a love triangle at Stony Brook and bribed doctors to lie about it in court. Miner's legal team hired Beatty to dig up Whitley's past in Boston.[41] The lines between federal law enforcement and the criminal underworld were hopelessly fluid.

As the Treasury squirmed, so did Miner. Lewis B. Whitney came to testify on December 20, 1871. Whitney was the officer who arrested Joshua D. Miner in Ohio in 1855, and when Whitney took the stand, Miner became agitated and got up from his seat. Miner's lawyers tried hard to convince the jury that Whitney had misidentified Miner from back in 1855, but Whitney stood firm. The best the defense team could do was point out that Whitney now ran a billiard saloon in Erie, Pennsylvania.

The government then brought out Philetus S. Bosworth, the deputy sheriff and jailer in Cleveland at the time Miner was arrested there. His tone had changed considerably from the time of Governor Chase's pardon.[42] Bosworth identified Miner from his 1855 incarceration and testified that he not only assisted in arresting Miner but also found $7,000 in counterfeit

Top: An 1863 large-denomination American Bank Note Company bill created using fiber paper shot through with "jute." *American Numismatic Association.*

Bottom: The back face of the 1863 $100 US Treasury bill created by the American Bank Note Company. Note forgery penalty. *American Numismatic Association.*

bills on him. Miller M. Spangler, the high sheriff in Cleveland in 1855, also identified Miner. Miner's lawyers responded with about a dozen witnesses either testifying about Miner's good character or the precise dimensions of the horse stable near the "dirt pile," in hopes of undermining the agents' credibility. The court adjourned on December 23, and the verdict was announced a few days after Christmas: not guilty.[43] Spectators in the courtroom applauded and "warmly" congratulated Joshua D. Miner.

A few weeks later, on January 30, 1872, Jot Miner was elected treasurer of the Nineteenth Assembly of the District Republican Association, as ordered by the Republican State Committee. "It is thus the Radicals of New York and elsewhere, punish crime," lamented the *Shelby County Democrat* on February 2.

6

LINCOLN

Banking on the Public

Lincoln did not enter the Civil War from a position of strength. The economies of the Northern and Southern states were too tightly intertwined: in his own Midwestern base, bankers relied on Southern financial securities as assets. No Midwestern banks were well enough managed to replace the role of Missouri's financial institutions. This situation translated into mediocre political support for Lincoln's military action.

How does one finance a war without bankers on one's side?

The answer to that question, in Lincoln's case, is the topic of this chapter. Lincoln was able to harness the power of inflation—a polite form of counterfeiting—to force bankers into political compliance or out of business.

Perhaps the strangest thing about Monroe's Bonelatta Gang was why they created fake \$100, \$500 and \$1,000 U.S. treasury bills during the foundation of the National Banking System. We should begin by asking ourselves, *How sure can we be that this information is accurate?* Treasury records of the Latta-related investigations are not available; however, accounts given by Secret Service operative Captain Patrick D. Tyrrell[1] match those of John. S. Dye, author of *The Government Blue-Book: A Complete History of the Lives of all the Great Counterfeiters* (1880), as well as contemporary press reports like that of *New York Daily Herald* on October 27, 1871.[2] What sources we have are from contemporary men who were likely to have been familiar with the Bonelatta investigation. These sources all agree that high-denomination bills were being counterfeited.

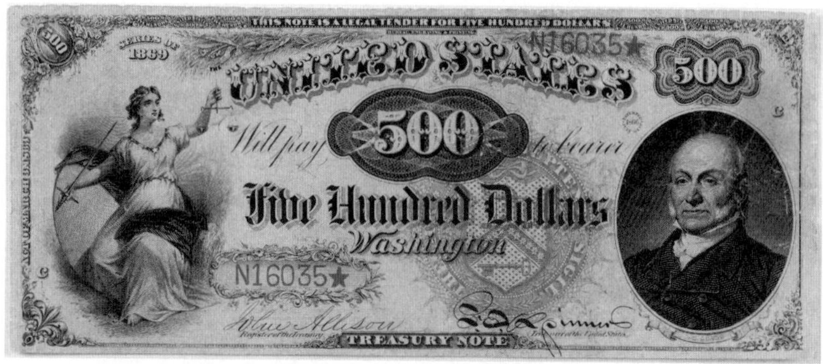

A $500 Treasury bill from 1869 (*top, front; bottom, back*). *Smithsonian Institution.*

In addition, the Treasury *did* print high-denomination bills, which were typically a wartime phenomena. By 1862, Lincoln had authorized the creation of $100, $500 and $1,000 denomination federal (Treasury) notes.[3]

Bear in mind that in the 1860s a well-to-do person could buy an upmarket house—multiple bedrooms with "a parlor and piazzas"—for $2,000 USD.[4] Daily necessities were measured in pennies. Regular people used coinage and small-denomination bills. Most counterfeiting crime was based on cheating low-information wage earners. These victims would likely never see a $100 bill in their life. Even in 1969, the $500 denomination was discontinued "due to lack of use."[5] So why counterfeit these huge denominations in the 1860s and '70s?

The first glimmer of an answer comes from Dye's *Government Blue-Book* and its account of Tom Ballard's creations (emphasis added):

> *A plate for counterfeiting the One Hundred and the Five Hundred Dollar Old Issue United States Treasury Notes, and an immense amount more*

> *of the same general description, just as the supposed emergencies of* **a vast scheme for counterfeiting the United States currency** *required...*
>
> *As the Government multiplied its Issues and enlarged its indebtedness, the presses of Hinman, Miner & Co, using the plates of Ballard,* **ran a race with the Treasury Department** *in the inflation of the currency.*[6]

Lincoln's super-high-denomination bills were designed for other bankers to use. In the lead-up to the war, Lincoln's Treasury Secretary, Salmon P. Chase, sprang from jail the man responsible for printing and distributing the Bonelatta high-denomination fakes. This man, Joshua D. Miner, set up industrial-scale Treasury note counterfeiting with at least one moonlighter educated by Chase's own Treasury Department, Tom Ballard. Why was the fox put in charge of the henhouse?

Lincoln's wartime financing plan required vast amounts of cash that the North wouldn't willingly give to him. If bankers could be surreptitiously taxed via inflation—in essence, if their consent and political agency were removed from the equation—then Lincoln could finagle paying for his war. Northern bankers would need to be forced to use new Lincoln-controlled bills in order for his scheme to work.

Readers may exclaim, "Such a devious scheme could only be dreamed up in the mind of a counterfeiter!" They would be half right. The scheme was dreamed up in the mind of a *counterfeiting watchdog*.

Portrait of John Thompson, publisher of the *Bank Note Reporter* and architect of Lincoln's wartime financing system. *Library of Congress.*

John Thompson, a recent bankrupt and publisher of *Bank Note Reporter*, was the architect of the modern U.S. government debt-financing system. As historian James Grant explains: "At the outbreak of war (US Civil War 1860), John Thompson, though surely distracted by his own affairs, nonetheless was able to participate in the national debate over how to organize the banking system to serve the Union cause."

Lincoln wasn't going to win the war without drastic action. As the Federal Reserve itself recounts:

> *In 1863, the United States was entering its third year of violent and costly fighting. Originally expected to be a short skirmish, the Civil War quickly developed into a full-blown military and industrial endeavor. The conflict required significant government spending, and despite large tax increases, the federal budget went from a surplus of $5.6 million before the war to a deficit of $423 million by 1862.*[7]

Thompson came to this desperate plan at a complicated time in his life. He had made his name by publishing *Thompson's Bank Note Reporter*, the preeminent publication alerting U.S. businessmen as to which notes in circulation were fake. This was a hugely powerful and dangerous position for a publisher to be in, especially so because Thompson was also a dealer in banknotes himself. The temptation to abuse his position must have been formidable. For example, this is the way the Thompsons checked a bank's balance sheet, according to James Grant:

> *As a check on the solvency of note-issuing banks Thompson had dispatched his sons in horse and buggy to present them with their own notes. To redeem one's notes was to pay gold coin for them. A bank that was incapable of meeting this demand was, prima facie, insolvent, and Thompson would fry it in his paper and perhaps precipitate its closing.*[8]

George Fisher Baker was recruited at a young age to be the front for John Thompson's financial schemes. *Library of Congress.*

Thompson went bankrupt during the Panic of 1857, yet he completed a palatial summer estate called The Anchorage in Highland, New York, during his bankruptcy. The final brick was laid the same year Joshua D. Miner left the Ohio Penitentiary for Fifty-Ninth Street, New York City.

John Thompson lobbied for the 1863 National Banking Act, an act that forced banks to use government-printed money as reserves instead of gold.[9] The act also gave the federal government the ability to sell war bonds and securities—an important point for Thompson. Thompson arranged that he would be the broker for these new federal war bonds via the First National Bank of the City of New York (FNBCNY).

Thompson's sons received the first banking charter in New York City under the 1863 Currency Act. At the head of their bank, they put an ambitious young man named George Fisher Baker, whom they picked up from the political entourage of William H. Seward.[10]

Through Seward, both Baker and his father[11] had become functionaries of patrician families like the Livingstons and van Rensselaers. Robert Livingston, the worst of the pimps, was busy building his NYC bordello empire when families like the Bakers were looking for new patronage as their traditional Quaker dons crumbled via factional infighting over the 1830s–40s.[12]

In light of the above, it's not surprising that Pa Baker was able to finagle a job for his son at the New York State Banking Department, remunerated at twice George's previous private sector salary. This was just the beginning of lucrative things to come.

George F. Baker used his government-affiliated post to become a financial intelligence and investing vehicle for his father. Playing U.S. government bonds was George's particular specialty, which brought him to the attention of John Thompson.

Whatever Thompson saw in the seventeen-year-old George Baker, Thompson saw it in the year he went bankrupt, 1857. Thompson and his sons invited young Baker to be a partner in "Thompson Brothers" and sold him stock in the outfit on credit. George's father agreed to this arrangement, and the Thompsons proceeded to use the boy as a front man for financial endeavors.[13]

One of these endeavors was the First National Bank of the City New York, which opened its doors on July 22, 1863, with twenty-three-year-old George F. Baker allegedly guiding its finances. Commercial moneylending was not this bank's goal; its goal was to shepherd the government bond market. From James Grant:

> *George F. Baker brought the asset of political pull to his job with the Thompsons. His father was an intimate of Secretary of State* [William H.] *Seward; and Seward, it was expected, would bring the merits of the new bank to the attention of Secretary to the Treasury Salmon P. Chase.*

Chase did precisely what was "expected," and in 1864 the FNBCNY became agent for the sale of the Union's 5 percent bonds—in other words, they were the first organization to profit from trading Lincoln's IOUs. Thompson didn't dine alone; Jay Cooke & Co. would also join the feeding frenzy.

John Cameron created this 1864 cartoon lampooning Lincon's war financing: "William Pitt Fessenden cranks out greenbacks from 'Chase's Patent Greenback Mill.'" Fessenden succeeded Salmon P. Chase as Treasury secretary. *Library of Congress.*

The National Banking Act was not a good deal for most bankers compared to what they enjoyed under the individual states' stewardship. National banks had to hold 25 percent of their deposits in "reserves" of greenbacks, and these greenbacks couldn't go into circulation.[14] Bank directors who didn't comply would be held personally liable and bankrupted.[15] National banks were restricted in their investments and prohibited from circumventing the greenback by issuing notes against land.[16] Remember that the greenback was being even more heavily inflated via Monroe, Wisconsin counterfeiting networks than was admitted by official printing numbers from the Treasury.

The difference between Lincoln's greenback and regular private-issue banknotes was that the Lincoln's money was not convertible into anything else. It was "legal tender" by force of law rather than by virtue of a healthy banking balance sheet. While this created a unified national currency, it also created a new risk: nationwide banking failures.

The state-chartered banks of New York and elsewhere resisted this federal colonization. Thompson, Lincoln and Chase needed a good public relations campaign. Their first move was to send a federal examiner named Charles A. Meigs to pump the reputation of the FNBCNY. Meigs trumpeted that FNBCNY's profits grew "without *precedent* in the history of banking in the City of New York."[17]

How did FNBCNY achieve these remarkable profits? By lending against U.S. government bonds. FNBCNY exploited having first access to legally mandated "capital" printed by Lincoln in order to lend to smaller banks in the hinterlands. Hence the eagerness of men like Arabut Ludlow to set up their own national banks—Ludlow's bank was only the 230th national charter issued among thousands. Meigs noted how the FNBCNY built business relationships with new national banks "in all parts of the United States and in fact it may well be called a Manufactory of National Banks."[18]

Meigs went on to say:

> *Almost all of their* [FNBCNY's] *Discounted Paper, they have discounted for their Country Correspondents, with the endorsement of the Bank from whom it was discounted, and, as a consequence, losses in this line are of very rare occurrence.*

This means that when national banks orbiting FNBCNY made bad loans, the Thompson brothers could jump in their buggy and make up the difference with newly printed greenbacks—or *possibly*, they could just have Bone Latta express package those otherwise unpassable high-denomination bills. These inflationary Bonelatta bills would be off books for the Treasury.

We are blessed to have an account of how FNBCNY's piles of "currency" made it to Lincoln's "correspondent" banks at the right time. In Meigs's own words:

> *I will cite the case of their correspondent— "the Rochester Savings Bank" with $8 Million Deposits— very sound—but upon whom a run was commenced about 10 days since.*
>
> *Two of the Trustees at once applied to the 1st National Bank for help—having 2 Million of U.S. and other good Bonds, in their hands.*
>
> *The Bank loaned them $500,000 Currency, on the spot, and hurried it to Rochester, by Express.*
>
> *Within a day or two $600,000 more was loaned them—in Currency—and hurried to Rochester—to the rescue of a solvent Institution! and a virtual agreement made to make the amount up to $2 Million, if needed—Securities to this amount being left in their hands....*

> *Now all this was done so quietly that the world knew not from whence the mighty "help" came.*
>
> *It is a great "feather in their cap" and I commend them for their energy of action at a time of most urgent need, and would offset this against some of their "Brokerage" business, as there is not a single Bank in our City who would or could have helped a country correspondent to such gigantic figures, and on such short notice!*
>
> *Can you wonder that this Institution gets such enormous Country Bank Deposits when this is the way they will come to the rescue?*[19]

Profiting from uncertainty around their satellite banks, from a federally subsidized position themselves, became the primary source of business for the FNBCNY. Grant:

> *In fat times, it (FNBCNY) accepted the deposits of country banks and paid them a small rate of interest, relending at a higher rate. In lean times, it would anticipate the role of the Federal Reserve System, standing ready to lend to a correspondent in trouble.*[20]

While federal examiner Meigs gushed about the FNBCNY business model, he struggled to say anything good about its accounting practices, which he described as "peculiar, but it is specially adapted to the nature of the business in which they are engaged." The real danger was having to account for bills on the books of satellite national banks that should not have been there according to Chase's Treasury.

In effect, the National Bank Acts of 1863–64 were the first way taxpayers were compelled to pay for national bankers' poor banking decisions. After all, Uncle Sam never fails because working people are alive to tax. But what sort of business climate does that make for bankers who didn't bend over for Lincoln? They lost a big chunk of their business (issuing their own bills) and had to bear financial responsibility for their banking failures. It was just a matter of time before nature took its course.

So what did the Thompsons do with all this currency? Buy more favors around Washington, D.C.!

> *A favorite investment of the First* [FNBCNY] *was the District of Columbia. "In looking over their affairs," wrote Meigs to the home office in March 1873* [when Grant had gently closed the Bonelattas], *"I find that over $6,500,000 of the bonds for the grading, paving,*

"Clubhouse of the Jekyll Island Club, once the winter preserve of New York's Union Club off Brunswick, Georgia." *Library of Congress.*

> *services, of your City has passed thro* [sic] *the hands of this Institution during the past two years!*"[21]

What guaranteed the preeminence of the FNBCNY was the Panic of 1873, which bankrupted its strongest competition. This panic was started by the Hapsburgs' "orgy of speculation" around railway development with "underworld" British investors and the Rothschilds.[22] The ripple effect of this liberal banking failure on other overheated rail investments—like Jay Cooke's Northern Pacific Railway—undid bankers whose teat wasn't solely the U.S. government. As one of the few big banks left standing, FNBCNY was set to become Citibank.[23] Most of the big names in American banking owe their success to being on the right side of national politics during the Civil War.

In 1877, the Thompson clan decided to distance themselves from Baker. They handed Baker, now thirty-seven years old, the FNBCNY and founded their new Chase National Bank two weeks later.[24] Chase National was named after Salmon P. Chase, who had died in 1873. Why the Thompsons divorced FNBCNY is unclear. However, while Thompson Sr. made a point of stating he left Baker's bank "sound as a nut," he also said that 1877 was a good year to start a bank without real estate, debts, lawsuits or cash problems.[25]

The history of banking in the United States is largely the history of how things kept getting sweeter for national banks. On December 23, 1913, when President Wilson signed the Federal Reserve Act in the rush up to Christmas, that sweetness reached a new apogee. Members of the Jekyll Island Club, which included George Fisher Baker, designed this act with the finances of warring Europe in their crosshairs.[26] Wartime is always "Baker weather,"[27] as club members dubbed good times for profit.

7
THE KENTUCKY COLONY

A great deal of Napoleon Bonaparte Latta's counterfeit money work was done in Chicago. He came to the attention of the Secret Service in Chicago, and by the testimony of Operative Lonergan, Latta appears to have been in Chicago at least once a month by 1871.

What did the counterfeit currency scene in the Windy City look like? A survey of contemporary press shows that fake New York bank bills were the most common, with distributors working the Ohio and Mississippi Rivers—exactly the footprint we would expect from the Bonelatta Gang. Violence between rival gangs is never mentioned. In the absence of systematic scholarship documenting Chicago's counterfeiting underworld in the 1850s–70s, the best we can say is that the Bonelattas appear to have been sophisticated players.

Other aspects of Chicago's criminal underworld at this time are well documented.[1] For example, the partnership between political elites and organized gambling is verifiable. By far the most successful clan in Chicago's history of government-sponsored organized crime is the Kentucky Colony, a syndicate of families who came from Louisville, Kentucky.

The Kentucky Colony has a connection with Monroe, Wisconsin, too. Tradition has it that Arabut Ludlow was friends with Potter Palmer, husband of the Colony's famous daughter Bertha Honoré Palmer. Ludlow's friendship extended to Palmer's business partner Marshall Field.[2] Palmer was a property developer along Chicago's State Street, while Marshall Field grew Palmer's mercantile business into State Street's iconic department store.[3]

Left: Potter Palmer, the famous Chicago merchant and real estate developer. Palmer was from a Quaker family in New Bedford, Massachusetts. *Wikipedia.*

Right: Marshall Field, the famous Chicago department store owner. For many years, Field rented his State Street premises from his retail mentor Potter Palmer. *Library of Congress.*

There are no known diaries or letters documenting these friendships. However, Monroe's chronicler of oral history, E.C. Hamilton, describes Palmer's friendship in some detail. Hamilton worked with Monroe's newspaper editor Emery A. Odell, who was in a position to know Ludlow's personal history:

> *In 1884, the biggest news story appearing in the "Sun" and "Sentinel" columns concerned completion of Arabut Ludlow's imposing four-story (including attic) brick hotel structure on the southeast corner of 16th Avenue and 9th Street. This massive Victorian Gothic style hotel, with its lavish interior furnishings (and one bathroom, at first, to each floor), was praised by townspeople and guests as one of the finest to be found west of Chicago. Ludlow's friendship with Potter Palmer, famed Chicago hotel builder, probably led him to spare no expense in trying to match the best to be found in that city.*[4]

The Chicago hotel described above is the Palmer House Hotel, which played a key role in Chicago's vice scene before 1910. The hotel was a

The Ludlow House Hotel, Monroe, Wisconsin. This hotel, pictured with the wires of 1884 "mod cons," was razed in the 1960s. *Author's collection.*

grooming ground for the prostitution dons and vote-harvesting kingpins popularly known as Lords of the Levee. Right now, let us examine the Kentucky Colony's founders.

It's a mystery why this tightly knit clan sold their Louisville plantations and slaves en masse in 1855 and traveled to the backwater of Chicago, Illinois. The most likely explanation for their exodus is that the families of the Kentucky Colony were involved in organized crime back home.

In 1853, when Colony families sent Henry Hamilton Honoré to scout a likely base on the outskirts of Chicago, Louisville was shaken by the disruption of the massive counterfeiting ring described in chapter 4. None of the politically connected ringleaders were prosecuted.

By the end of the Civil War, Chicago was swamped in organized vice,[5] and the Kentucky Colony controlled the city's Democratic Party and city services. The Colony did this either through bribery or appointing reliable men to positions of trust inside the police, judiciary and so on. Colony

Left: Henry Hamilton Honoré was the behind-the-scenes leader of the early Kentucky Colony in Chicago. *Cyclopaedia of American Biography, 1918.*

Right: Carter Harrison IV, the second Chicago mayor from the Harrison family and coauthor of *Chicago Yesterdays*. *Chicago History Museum.*

families became masters at manipulating ethnic grievances and ginning up mob violence to reach their political goals. Their crowning achievement was the 1893 Columbian Exposition and Chicago's second vice wave over 1891–1910.

Most of what we know about the Kentucky families was shaped by the political needs of their famous sons, Mayor Carter H. Harrison III (1825–1893) and Mayor Carter H. Harrison IV (1860–1953). All sources describe an initial property purchase by Henry Hamilton Honoré in 1853, which represents the colony aspect of the clique's name.[6] The families then built interlocking estates on this vast track of land, replicas of the luxuriant plantations they left back home.

Who were these Kentucky Colony families? Carter Harrison IV published a list of them: the Harrisons and Henry Honoré's clan, Judge John G. Rogers, Judge Samuel M. Moore, Judge Murray F. Tuley, John E. Owsley, A.C. Badger, one "Colonel Winchester" and finally the family of Judge

Buckner Stith Morris (second mayor of Chicago).[7] Harrison notes that "all were Kentuckians and prominent in the early business and political history of the city."[8]

There were three families who were not Kentuckians but were still considered part of the Colony, as "they had many characteristics of that strong race." These were the families of S.S. Hayes; the Waller brothers (construction industry partners); and finally W.S. Bryan, the political scientist cousin of William Jennings Bryan.[9]

When the Honorés moved to fashionable Michigan Avenue in 1866, the Harrisons bought their house and preserved the congruity of the base. The Harrisons lived there until 1904, with only a brief intermission between 1873 and 1876, when they lived in German Europe. (Prior to this, in the 1850s, Carter Harrison III had spent time in Paris befriending socialists and down-and-out 1848 revolutionaries in cafés.)[10]

By 1878, Arabut Ludlow owned the land across Ashland Avenue from the Colony base, having grown wealthy when Monroe, Wisconsin, was the nation's distribution headquarters for forged banknotes.[11]

What was the Colony's base like? Harrison IV describes it:

> *The homes of the Honoré, Winchester, Owsley, and Harrison families had grounds covering the entire blocks on which they were located. These Kentuckians were farmers' boys; plenty of space and fresh air were necessities to them. On their grounds they kept their horses, cows, and chickens, and here they had their gardens in which all the family vegetables were raised.*

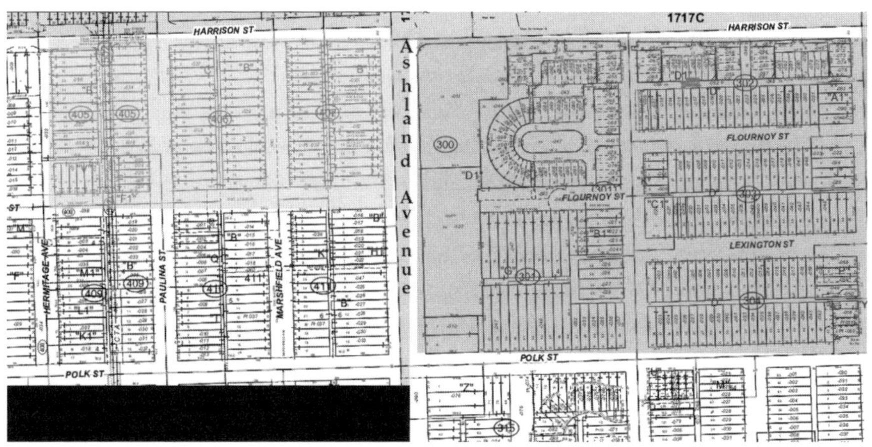

2021 Sidwell Maps number 1717E superimposed onto 1718H. Ludlow's 1878 property is the shaded LHS block across Ashland Avenue, while the Colony base is the shaded RHS. *Cook County, Illinois (Tax Maps).*

Harrison IV describes a circuit of dance parties in the ballrooms of these homes and buffets groaning under the weight of dusty grapes from Spain or the precious citrus fruits that would later preoccupy Bertha Honoré Palmer in Florida. This expansive lifestyle was at odds to their long-settled neighbors, as Harrison IV explains:

> *There were then seven houses in Reuben Street* [Ashland Boulevard]. *One of these was "the chicken- woman's", at the southwest corner of Reuben and Monroe streets. She probably had another name, a good old Irish patronymic on the order of O'Brien, McInerney or Gallagher: I did not know it. She was "the chicken-woman" to all of us. Her home, an eye-sore to the neighborhood, was a tumble-down frame shack, fenced in with a dilapidated barricade originally intended to keep her two cows, her goats, and her geese within an enclosure, but which, long since fallen to pieces, had ceased to serve its purpose.*

From his youngest days, Harrison IV remembered a sort of separateness about his life as part of the Kentucky Colony, for example, he contrasts "Kentuckians" with the "Micks"—Irish boys who were jealous of Kentucky kids' ice skates. (Harrison IV opined that many of these "Micks" now worked for him on Chicago's police force.) "Kentuckians" would also watch German *Turngemeinde* parades from the vantage of their upper-story windows.[12]

There was a certain amount of tension inside the Colony, too:

> *As a child I used to hear an interesting story connected with the building of the old* [Honoré] *home. The building was up, the roof almost shingled when, for some reason, the carpenters quit work. Whether it was a forerunner of the modern strike, the result of a disagreement, or just an ordinary laying down of the tools on a job, I do not know. It is enough for the purpose of the story that the men stopped their labors while the roof remained incomplete. A thunderstorm was brewing. Black clouds lay off in the southwest, darkening the skies. It was important that the shingling of the roof be completed before the storm should break. So in good, neighborly, whole-souled Kentucky fashion, Mr. Honoré commandeered the services of his friends, among whom were Colonel Winchester, John G. Rogers, and my father. Off went coats and collars and in a short while the remaining shingles were laid and the roofing completed.*
>
> *Now comes the nub of the story. While the work was in progress, at the corner of Reuben and Harrison streets, only three blocks away, the*

> *sheriff of Cook County was publicly executing a criminal, and Mr. Honoré furnished his guests with an opera-glass that they might take turns in watching proceedings and, incidentally, that he might keep them on the job!*

The clannish nature of the Colony families contributed to their remarkable political rise, a rise that Chicago's German settlers compared to "rapine."[13] By the time of the Civil War, Lincoln's partisans at Joseph Medill's *Chicago Tribune* saw the city's Kentucky Colony as a two-headed snake:

> *The Kentucky colony in Chicago is still subject to habeas corpus. Kentucky loyalty is noble. Kentucky disloyalty is the very cobra type of Copperheadism. But while our home traitors in Chicago can only harmlessly wriggle and hiss, they are dangerous in Kentucky, as the President has found out, and he has brought his foot down upon them.*[14]

Naturally, the *Chicago Tribune* took a public stance against its Democrat rivals. However, while the public image of the Colony was staunchly Democrat, in reality they were happy to work with Democrats and Republicans alike. H. Honoré's second daughter married Ulysses Grant's son, and Bertha helped with Grant's presidential campaigns.

Accusations of corruption against the Colony had become quite serious by 1876, when the Harrison family returned from central Europe. *Chicago Tribune* writers reported[15] the discovery of a circular explaining how a franchise of the "Democratic Kentucky colony is to be imported in that state [Indiana]." This franchise was staffed by an army of "tramps" and railway workers who were imported into key city wards to throw the vote in favor of presidential hopeful Samuel Tilden.

In Chicago's press, "colonizing" became a word for the type of political corruption that exploited pseudo-charity to buy votes from low-cost labor. As time passed, the success of the Colony's tactics alienated swing voters, especially those in Chicago's German community, who saw crime run rampant and their interests shunted. This is a translation of an editorial approved by Washington Hesing in the *Illinois Staats-Zeitung* prior to November 21, 1881:

> *What has not been attempted for twenty years this side of the Alleghenies in any large or small cities in which more than one language is recognized—to ostracize the German language in an official manner—in this city, whose population is one-third German, has been accomplished by the Kentucky*

> *demagogue who, as quasi-Irishman, has a claim to the name McHarrison* [Carter Harrison III]*….McHarrison belongs to this vilely-known and ill-reputed Kentucky colony for whom Chicago was a field for rapine, the same as Deadwood, in Dakota, or Tombstone, in Arizona, are for the adventuresome Eastern capitalist of today.*[16]

The *Staats-Zeitung* spelled out the corruption problem in this 1881 article, which was reprinted by the *Chicago Tribune* on April 7, 1885:

> *The renomination of Harrison for Mayor surprised nobody, since it was predetermined. The Democratic party in Chicago has no hopes of success if it does not use those dishonest means which Harrison's control of the police, fireman, street-laborers, etc., puts at his disposal….All remember how Mr. Harrison at the last November election* [1880], *through his appeal to the laboring classes, incited them to Ku-Klux acts of violence. That the attempt failed does not lessen its criminality.*[17]

History has come down on the side of the above *Staats-Zeitung* editor: Harrison did buy the Democratic Party through a system of patronage and bribery with vice money, a system that was christened "bossism."

German leaders, like the publishers of the *Staats-Zeitung*, understood bossism too. The aforementioned clippings, both from 1881, show how critical German Chicago's leading newspaper was toward the Colony and Carter Harrison III. This criticism suddenly turned to support in 1884. The about-face was so absurd that Chicago's other German paper, the *Freie-Presse*, published articles lampooning behavior of *Staats-Zeitung*'s editors.[18]

What had happened with Chicago's German leaders? We must look to central European state security for answers.

The *Illinois Staats-Zeitung* was a venerable paper in Chicago that had been owned by the Brentano family for the duration of the Civil War. The Brentanos were a merchant family who enjoyed special favor from the Landgraviate of Hesse-Darmstadt. By the time of Darmstadt's spymaster Johann Heinrich Merck's career, the Brentanos were involved in literary propaganda.[19] (Merck was pro–French Revolution and had set up a network of literary propagandists.) In 1862, during the Civil War, the Brentanos went into business with Washington Hesing's father, Anton "Boss" Hesing, to manage their newspaper in Chicago.[20]

Life was difficult in German Europe. A series of revolutions[21] whereby liberals—often wealthy merchants like the Brentanos[22]—hoped to wrest

Left: Carter Harrison III, a charismatic politician whose popular appeal was matched only by his lack of ethics. *Library of Congress.*

Right: Anton Hesing was Cook County sheriff shortly after Allan Pinkerton. He joint-owned the *Illinois Staats-Zeitung* with the Brentano family and was a Republican political boss. *Wikipedia.*

power from their respective rulers resulted in the Hohenzollern family (Imperial Prussia) becoming the most powerful rulers in Europe. "Liberal" or socialist agitators were exiled to places like Chicago, while organized crime and pseudo-revolutionaries benefited from appeasement via economic favoritism. German Europe had jumped out of the frying pan and into the fire.

During the 1850s, Prussia's ruler Frederick Wilhelm IV established a police force who watched international revolutionaries. Clandestine police forces were adopted throughout Europe, but in Prussia this apparatus was headed by Wilhelm J.C.E. Stieber, who was a genius at using criminal networks to fight crime.

One of Stieber's first charges was to contain Karl Marx's cell in London, the International Communist League.[23] Socialist agitators were using democratic institutions to instigate revolts; sometimes these agitators were financed by governments in order to destabilize competitors—Prussia was active this way.[24] Karl Marx himself was never too far from sympathetic spies like Austrian agent Heinrich Börnstein[25] or the Prussian Adalbert von Bornstedt.[26] (Marx was also European correspondent for Horace Greeley's *New York Tribune*!)[27] By 1870, Marx and socialism had been good to the Hohenzollerns.[28]

Stieber was observant and noticed something about Marx's agents:

> *The members of the German, as well as the foreign, Communist leagues were mostly German, and the command center in London consisted exclusively of German emigrants, most of whom belonged to literary circles.*[29]

Stieber was not alone in this observation. Scholars have noted a preponderance of German last names among the early revolutionaries in Imperial Russia, too.[30] Small wonder then that by 1873 Chicago was experiencing the same revolutionary problems. Historian Fred Schied describes how *Arbeiter-Vereine* (workers' associations) set up by German immigrants nurtured socialism in Chicago:

> *From the late 1850s until after the Haymarket Affair in 1886, the Arbeiter-Vereine were at the center of a vigorous cultural and social movement which shaped and significantly influenced the course of American radicalism.... Radical European socialist thought was introduced to American society through German working-class organizations such as the Arbeiter-Vereine.*[31]

German immigrants made up one-third of Chicago's population, and their cultural clubs were "the focal point for organizing demonstrations and political action."[32] Turner Halls (*Turngemeinde*) played a similar political role, though less overtly socialist.[33] Consequently, these clubs attracted German intelligence operatives working, and watching, in the United States.

Joseph Weydemeyer was a Prussian soldier who propagandized for Karl Marx. He served with the Union army during the U.S. Civil War. *Wikipedia.*

In light of their espionage potential, it shouldn't be surprising that Chicago's *Arbeiter-Vereine* became soapboxes for men like Joseph Weydemeyer, "a former lieutenant in the Prussian army who met Karl Marx in Cologne when Marx was the editor of the *Rheinische Zeitung*."[34] Marx told Weydemeyer to spread his message in Chicago.

This foreign interference wasn't lost on native-born Americans, and on Christmas Day 1873, the *Chicago Tribune* ran a front-page exposé covering "Our Communists" and the Marxist *Arbeiter-Verein*.[35] When Carter Harrison III dropped everything in 1873 for a three-year stint in German Europe, he entered the beating heart of the international communist movement as well as the espionage apparatus designed to harness it. This 'vacation' was a working one: Harrison III was reelected to Congress in 1876 having stumped from German Europe.[36]

Chicago's leaders, including the Colony, were motivated to address the socialism problem just as the Prussian emperor was. Through the insight of men like Stieber, German rulers learned how to co-opt socialism and organized crime to crush political dissent. This is exactly the strategy the Colony would use in Chicago after Carter Harrison III's return from his Central European sojourn. Historian James Green summarizes Harrison's political agenda:

> *A few businessmen and bankers realized, however, that Mayor Harrison had exhibited rare political genius following his election in 1879. He had co-opted leading socialists into his administration. He then created a labor-friendly regime that helped cast the Socialistic Labor Party into oblivion.*[37]

Chicago's *Arbeiter-Verein* problem was neutralized by the Haymarket Affair, which Mayor Harrison had an unsavory role in provoking. The murder of policemen by an enraged socialist mob, shortly after being whipped up by Harrison, turned public opinion against Chicago's immigrant workers.

Can we relate any of this to the counterfeiting problem in Chicago? Stieber believed currency counterfeiting supported revolutionary activity. He saw that Prussia's counterfeiting problems came from the same Rheinish area as Marx and Engels. Stieber claims he employed those same Rheinish counterfeiters to pay his network of spies in Austria.[38]

By the 1870s, Stieber had developed other tricks for managing political activists that were of interest to the Colony. Stieber initiated a system in Berlin where police took charge of pimping networks in exchange for protection and information on (political) criminals. Previously, these pimps ran *kompromat* factories staffed with child prostitutes and aimed at highly placed Prussian officials.[39]

Stieber's tactics were not wholly new. Under post-1848 Austrian police regimes in Hungary, pimping networks like Stieber's were key to undoing revolutionary leaders who, for some reason, were often in the company of pimps. By partnering with the criminal element in rebellious provinces like Hungary, the Hapsburgs were able to corrupt democratic institutions and keep power.[40] Eastern European (often Jewish) pimps were employed in the same manner as the American Pinkertons to break up political rallies that frightened the Hapsburgs or Romanovs.[41]

After the Harrison's German trip, the Colony embraced central European–style organized crime–based governance. In turn, their political cronies worked with German leaders to solve mutual problems. For instance, when Ulysses S. Grant assumed the presidency, he appointed a Unitarian and pro-Lincoln Democrat as ambassador to Berlin: George Bancroft.

A pressing issue between Berlin and Washington, D.C., was that German men immigrated to the United States to avoid conscription. The "Bancroft Treaties" arranged for the naturalization of these German subjects in the United States, subject to the military needs of Prussia. Chicago was a hotbed of the problems, or opportunities, presented to American leaders as a result of central Europe's human trafficking crisis.

The trafficking problem in Austria-Hungary was doubly complex because Austro-Hungarian organized crime dominated procuring women for the global sex trade. Vienna, like Chicago under the Colony, effectively legalized the sex trade by giving the police control over which bordellos could operate, a situation termed "tolerated prostitution."[42] In Chicago, favored pimps then organized election-rigging.

The role of police under tolerated prostitution is important to understand. The police were transformed into vice enforcers, rather than law enforcers. The police of nineteenth-century American cities were usually drawn from the same ethnic milieus as the criminals, making corruption problems even more tenacious.[43] Native-born Americans and law-abiding immigrants alike were held hostage to a mass immigration system that benefited only a small group of urban industrialists and their political machines.

Franz Joseph, emperor of Austria-Hungary. *Library of Congress.*

The result of tolerated prostitution in Eastern Europe was massive institutionalized corruption. Carter Harrison III would have looked into the eyes of Emperor Franz Joseph and seen a man he could understand.

Carter Harrison III wasn't the only American politician with this understanding. Prominent New York families, such as the Astors and Livingstons, had made similar vice deals in order to preserve their political power.[44] New York City's Tammany Hall operated on the proceeds of prostitution. In fact, it was a Lincoln man from Chicago's sphere who rose to power in New York City during the decade following the Civil War vice boom: President Ulysses S. Grant.

While Carter Harrison III was politicking in Berlin and Vienna, President Grant's son Frederick Dent Grant married a Kentucky Colony girl: Ida Marie Honoré. Ida was Bertha Palmer's sister. Having failed in New York politics in 1889, Frederick Dent Grant was assigned to Vienna as U.S. ambassador by President Benjamin Harrison, a relative of the Colony Harrisons. According to the account given by Bertha Palmer's heirs in *Silhouette in Diamonds*, the Grant couple were a favorite at Franz Joseph's court[45] and after their return to the United States in 1893, F.D. Grant was appointed police commissioner in New York City.

As NYC police commissioner, F.D. Grant served alongside politician Theodore Roosevelt, who made his career by "reforming" the tenements from which Austria-Hungary's gangsters worked in the United States.

President Harrison subsequently appointed Bertha Palmer to be the female president of the 1893 Columbian Exposition, a Congress-mandated celebration of national achievement. The exposition corresponded with a massive boom in Chicago sex tourism,[46] second only to the Civil War disaster. This new wave included both sex workers and gangsters from Austria-Hungary (particularly Galicia, in modern Poland). Chicago was wide open for Vienna's state-sponsored crime problem.

8

THE SONS OF LIBERTY

A few doors down from the nameless Irish "chicken lady" on Ashland Avenue lived another Irishman whom Carter Harrison IV would have remembered from his childhood, though Harrison chose not to mention him in *Chicago Yesterdays*. That Irishman was Michael McDonald, the "gambler king" and crime boss of Chicago, whose network of corruption made Carter Harrison III's political career possible.

During the U.S. Civil War, while Bone Latta hit his stride in Monroe, Wisconsin, a transformation took place in Chicago. What was once an English-style town on the prairie turned into a vice-ridden metropolis. The railroads pulled in miscreants from the Northeast, Mississippi River and Canada who then bribed police.

Chicago's head rotted next. The war ushered in an explosion of prostitution, the money from which underwrote crooked aldermen. According to historian Richard C. Lindberg,[1] the immediate cause of this collapse was the misrule of Mayor John Blake Rice, a theater magnate, whose administration collaborated with gangsters following legislation that disempowered the mayor's office and made the police answerable to a toothless commission. Civic funding and control of the Board of Public Works was transferred to the aldermen, who used it fund their henchmen.

Chicago wasn't alone in its nightmare. The war had kicked off the era of bossism, in which industrial towns like Chicago, New York City and San Francisco were taken over by "big city Democratic machines," as Lindberg terms them. This is only half the story though, because behind the bosses

Left: Mayor John Blake Rice: actor, theater manager and Lincoln Republican politician. *Wikipedia.*

Right: Michael McDonald, Chicago's first modern crime boss and "gambler king." *Chicago History Museum.*

like McDonald were cartels of respectable businessmen, the "Chicago Board of Trade men and State Street magnates." These magnates owned the Republican Party too, and politics became a game of playing constituents against each other.

One man who shone a light on the bosses behind the bosses was Missouri's Governor Joseph Wingate Folk (1905–9), himself a Democrat. Folk chose to fight Missouri's "culture of corruption." From Folk's biographer Kenneth H. Winn:

> *In the process of prosecuting corrupt politicians, however, he* [Folk] *made an important discovery. They all had ties to businessmen—rich ones. Many of the city's social elite lived in nice mansions in the city's Central West End. They became collectively known as the "Big Cinch." They owned banks, speculated in real estate, ran corporations, and were powerful lawyers. But here matters got more complicated. Their work gave them extensive business dealings with government. Many of these businessmen were shamelessly greedy, looking for the special privileges that only government could bestow.*[2]

Chicago was much like the St. Louis described above. The powerful urban businessmen had their own investment culture. In New York, for instance, families like the Livingstons, Astors or Lorillards liked to invest in prostitution by owning the tenements where madams set up shop. The most profitable and exclusive of these establishments would be located within easy distance of a fashionable flagship hotel, like the Astor's Waldorf-Astoria. East Coast potentates set the pattern for new money out West like the Honorés.

Mike McDonald, however, symbolized a different type of influence in Chicago. McDonald's inspiration came upward from New Orleans and its cesspool of legalized gambling. It was gambling, rather than prostitution, that was the bedrock of McDonald's fortune, though he taxed pimps too. The story of how Mike became Chicago's "Gambler King" is both terrifying and informative.

McDonald was born in County Cork, Ireland. His parents immigrated to the U.S. side of Niagara Falls, where his father became a day laborer. Whiskey problems led to an unhappy domestic life, and in the fall of 1854, at fifteen years old, Mike McDonald left home to become a "candy butcher" on the Michigan Central Railway, which linked Niagara to Chicago. Candy butchers were contracted by the railway to sell diversions to passengers; the butchers were often immigrant Irish boys, orphans or runaways. Mike was on the fast train to a life of organized crime.

Mike worked the passenger lines around Chicago practicing small-time confidence games. He spent his free hours charming local firemen, much older men than himself, with his abilities as a raconteur and card shark. By twenty-one (1859), he'd somehow found the cash to set up shop in New Orleans with a buddy named Roger Sherman.

Sherman and McDonald opened a gambling "agency" inside the luxuriant St. Charles Hotel on Canal Street under the guise of selling stereoscopic viewing devices. The real money was made betting in the hotel's anterooms. That the two young Northerners beat out New Orleans' two thousand other professional gamblers for the opportunity to fleece wealthy hotel patrons suggests formidable Southern underworld contacts. Lindberg:

> *New Orleans, with its sublime glamour, reputation for extravagant living, and air of wickedness left a lasting impression on Mike, affording him a privileged glimpse into a world that stirred his feverish imagination. Here, before him, stretched America's first "wide open" city; a raucous, sweltering cesspool where vice reigned supreme and alliances with sympathetic politicians made it possible for smart fellows to come out ahead.*[3]

Sherman's big mouth brought their bonanza to an end. Sherman got in a fight and made his "hothead abolitionist" sympathies known. Confederate regulars raided the hotel to arrest Sherman and McDonald. McDonald's quick tongue saved him, and without concern for the fate of Sherman, he ran back up to Niagara Falls to let things cool down.

Late 1861 found Mike back in Chicago, ready to exploit the tricks he'd picked up in New Orleans. However, Chicago was already a northern migration point for the "blackleg" gambling fraternity who slithered their way up and down the Mississippi.

A stereograph of the St. Charles Hotel on Canal Street in New Orleans, Louisiana. The hotel is the white building. *Library of Congress.*

It is an injustice to call these blacklegs "Southern" because they were as traitorous to the Confederacy in New Orleans as they were to the Union in Chicago. They were narcissistic confidence men with charisma. As forerunners to the 1890s dandies, blackleg culture necessitated a romantic style of dress: black broadcloth coats and white lace shirts offset with the largest diamond pin, or "headlight," that the rascal could afford. They lived a lifestyle similar to pimps, sponging off women by exploiting unrequited love. Their character did not change just because there was a war on:

Major General Benjamin Franklin Butler, a Massachusetts politician and Radical Republican. *Library of Congress.*

> *In April 1862, with Admiral David Farragut's fleet pummeling Confederate forts on the Mississippi, the gamblers formed their own volunteer company, the Wilson Rangers, or "Blackleg Cavalry," and served the cause unenthusiastically for less than three weeks before turning and running the face of superior firepower....*
>
> *Their services voluntarily ended, a faction of the Rangers and sporting men of New Orleans made convenient alliances with the occupying Federals, paid a stiff "street tax" for the privilege of operating, and took in the brother of Union general Benjamin F. Butler as a full salaried partner. Many more refugee blacklegs filtered north to avoid conscription, imprisonment or harassment by the Union occupiers.*[4]

When McDonald returned to Chicago in late 1861, there were already crime lords running their gambling hells and saloons. These lords were undisciplined and did not leverage their political contacts. The most famous lords were a Virginia native named George Trussell and Samuel H. "Cap" Hyman. They burnt themselves up via shoot-outs, dissipated living and eventually syphilis. That last problem became more pronounced with the advent of war because prostitution in Chicago exploded. This development was particularly noxious to Chicago's upright citizens.

McDonald understood that visible prostitution endangered gambling profits; the two rackets had to be kept separate. This "Chinese Wall"–style division eventually led to an ethnic bifurcation in Chicago's crime world:

> *Control of the segregated brothel districts proliferating in urban American in the second half of the nineteenth century gradually shifted away from Southerners and men and women with Anglo-Saxon surnames. Prostitution was mostly abandoned and left to the Russian Jews, Italians,*

> *and various Eastern Europeans arriving later in the squalid tenement districts of the big cities.*[5]

This was not to say that Irish, English or native-born Americans weren't involved in prostitution—both Hyman and Trussell's squeezes were madames. Prostitution was not the lifeblood of their business, however, as it was for the Austro-Hungarian gangsters for whom the Civil War would make room.

Where does counterfeiting fit into all this? Counterfeiters were the aristocrats of criminals, but they haunted the same saloons as their criminal brethren. Latta probably visited more than one saloon on his trips to Chicago and would have rubbed shoulders with men like McDonald. By the late 1860s, Latta would *have* to keep McDonald, or one of his lieutenants, happy. But how did McDonald achieve this position?

Fresh from Niagara Falls in 1861, Mike McDonald immediately diversified his gambling operations with a "bounty-jumping" con, meaning he would help a network of men enlist with the Union army to receive their signing-on bonus, then run away and reenlist somewhere else. The harvested bonuses would then be split among all members of the ring. This gig financed another hotel operation for McDonald: running the bar at the allegedly Copperhead Richmond House.

"Copperhead" was a pejorative term for Northern Democrat voters who sympathized with the South. Copperheads included Southerners in the North as well as immigrant Irish and German workers—often social reform–minded political refugees—who had an inconvenient regard for the Constitution that guaranteed the South their right to secede. These immigrants also tended toward more liberal social views, seeing prostitution and drunkenness as necessary evils.

Copperheads were rarely abolitionists: for them, granting manumission and the right to vote to formerly enslaved Black men was a bad deal. Indeed it was precisely these immigrants' wages that were depressed, their working conditions degraded and the power of their votes diminished when Yankee employers relocated Southern Blacks northward.

From a historical perspective, everything about McDonald's Copperhead Richmond House smells off. The hotel was built in 1856 by Thomas Richmond, a Chicago Board of Trade founder and early sponsor of Abraham Lincoln.[6] Richmond was an outspoken abolitionist and temperance man who moved to Chicago after a failed political career in Ohio. He was also a spiritualist: ghosts goaded Richmond's abolitionist fervor and led him to write his manifesto, *God Dealing With Slavery: God's Instrumentalities in Emancipating the African Slave in America.* So how did an edgy bar in Chicago get Richmond's surname and become a Copperhead hangout?

Thomas Richmond, Lincoln patron and founder of the Chicago Board of Trade. *William Noack (via Flickr, CC BY-ND 2.0).*

Prior to his legal career, Abraham Lincoln was also whiskey dealer: this was a shady enough venture for him to mislead people about it during his presidential campaign.[7] Like any subculture with widespread disapproval, whiskey sellers were clannish. Mike McDonald's bar at the Richmond House was co-financed by a whiskey dealer named Calvin P. Paige. The abolitionist magnates who could get behind an old whiskey man like Lincoln didn't need ethical consistency if money was at stake.

In his role behind the bar, McDonald's charisma paid off. Richmond House attracted the sporting type looking for "down-home Southern hospitality." A man could bet on horse races from its public rooms as well as mingle with crooks or refined businessmen. McDonald stood watch over the type of place a counterfeiter would appreciate: an information clearinghouse.

And information was plentiful. McDonald groomed a private army of con men to canvas railway stations and hotel lobbies looking for men who would be easy to fleece. They called marks "grangers," and grangers were the same sort of person Latta's shovers targeted. Grangers were low-hanging fruit, however.

Among the more edgy guests at the Richmond House were the Sons of Liberty. This group was allegedly a sleeper cell of Southern soldiers directed by Jacob Thompson, the former secretary of war under President James Buchanan. Their men included Copperhead sympathizers and scores of Canadian expatriates. We know that these Canadians entered the United States through Windsor, Ontario, a hub of the Underground Railroad smuggling network.[8]

The goal of this international band of conspirators was, allegedly, to break free Confederate soldiers from Camp Douglas, a prisoner-of-war camp. Camp Douglas was known as the "Andersonville of the North."[9] At the same time, the Sons of Liberty allegedly planned to disrupt the 1864

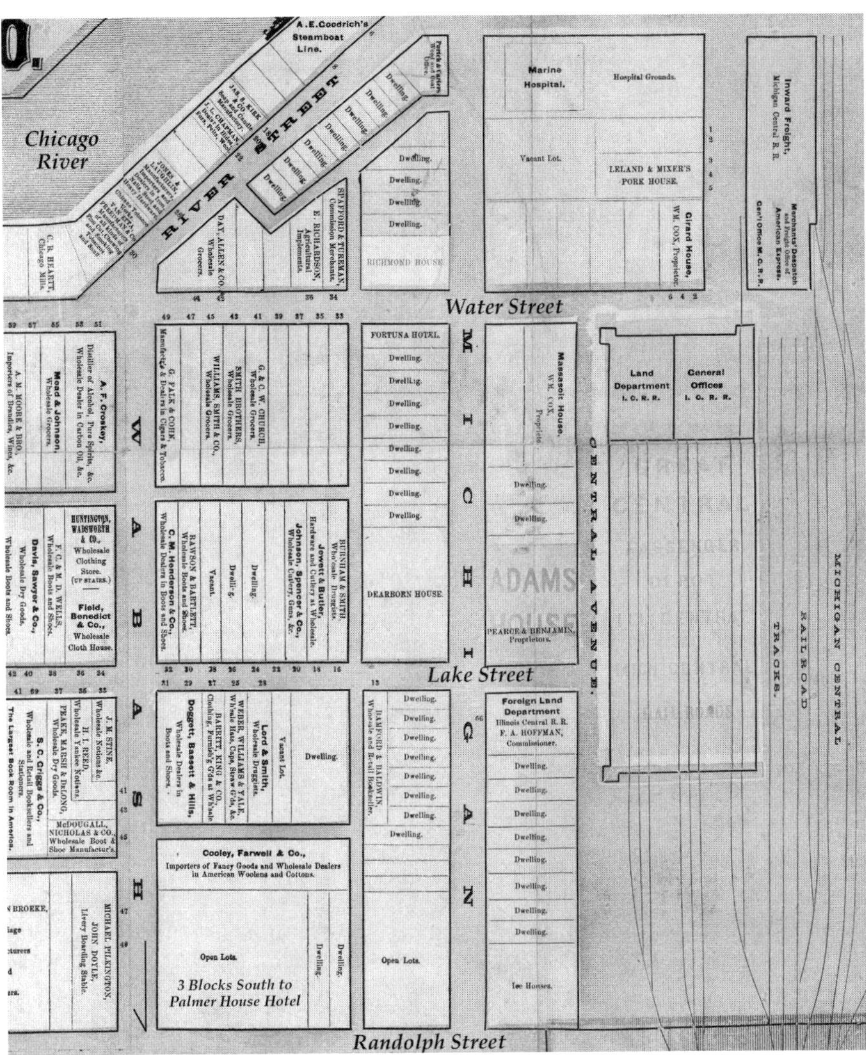

This portion of the 1862 "Map of the Business Portion of Chicago" shows Richmond house in Chicago's First Ward (shaded). *Prepared by E. Whitefield for the map-making concern of Rufus Blanchard, Public Domain, via Wikimedia Commons/ Chicago Historical Society.*

Democratic Convention and somehow thereby lead the Midwest to join the Confederacy. It's all rather fuzzy.

The attack was preempted by Union Colonel Benjamin J. Sweet just two days before the planned action, thanks to well-placed moles. We cannot be sure how involved McDonald was with organizing the attack, but we do know that McDonald was close with the plot's ringleaders, Bernard Caufield, Swayne Wickersham and James Geary, the arms dealer:

> *Among the rebel plotters were a handful of men who would go on to become standard-bearers of the Cook County* [Chicago] *Democratic Party in the postwar Reconstruction era: Congressman Bernard G. Caulfield for one, and Dr. Swayne Wickersham, a McDonald man elected First Ward alderman in 1879 and elevated to the chairmanship of the powerful Finance Committee and then city health commissioner. He was an important behind-the-scenes operative appointed by McDonald to numerous party caucuses and state nominating conventions in the 1870s–90s. They were to become important political allies and powerful party spokesmen when the Democrats challenged Ulysses S. Grant in 1868 with a candidate championing the saloon interests, espousing a segregationist point of view, and rebuking any president "who is not in favor of a white man's government; know-nothings who will pass a law requiring that a foreigner shall live in this country twenty-one years before he is entitled to vote...and place it* [the vote] *in the hands of the negro."* [10]

Bernard G. Caulfield, United States Representative from Illinois. *Library of Congress.*

McDonald closed his bar for renovations several months before the attack, thereby distancing himself from the Sons. If McDonald was genuinely in on the plan, was it smart for him to let its leaders work from his loudly Copperhead bar?

While the Sons of Liberty did patronize the Richmond House, the majority of the planning was done from 176 South Clark Street (the northwest corner of Clark and Monroe Streets), which lies two blocks west of the Palmer House Hotel site on State Street and Monroe. After the plot was foiled, McDonald developed 176 South Clark Street into a "department store for gambling" named "The Store." He was not tied up in the prosecution of the Sons, and his gambling business grew exponentially with ever greater lenience from authorities.

Only three out of about three hundred Sons defendants were convicted. What was going on? In a climate where pro-Lincoln politicians would

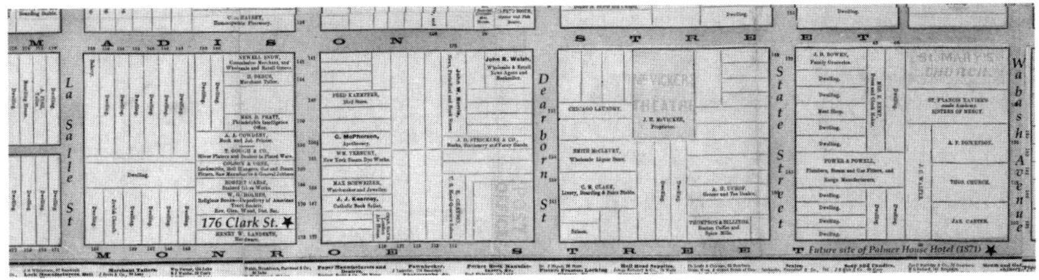

An 1862 Chicago map showing where the "Sons of Liberty" operation was planned at 176 Clark Street, which became Mike McDonald's "department store of gambling." *Prepared by E. Whitefield for the map-making concern of Rufus Blanchard, Public Domain, via Wikimedia Commons/ Chicago Historical Society.*

torture their neighbors for disunion views, why were the Sons of Liberty treated so gently?

One answer may be that the Sons were managed opposition who gave Lincoln men an excuse to crush political and mob-world competitors.

Our knowledge of Monroe, Wisconsin's role in the Bonelatta's Treasury-sponsored counterfeiting ring *may* also provide insight. Arabut Ludlow couldn't have continued to profit from Bone Latta's business supplying Samuel Chase with counterfeit treasury notes if Illinois' government shifted Democrat and the war ended. McDonald's Kentucky Colony neighbors were making too much money to let that happen. Instead, the Copperhead bust freed McDonald up to concentrate on electing Colony mayors like Carter Harrison III.

McDonald's usefulness to Carter Harrison III depended on McDonald's ability to coerce working people into voting the right way. The base unit of McDonald's *political* criminal empire was selling the votes of Twentieth Ward inhabitants.

The Twentieth Ward is the voting district that sits north of the Chicago River. Below it, on the river's south bank, lies the First Ward and south of that the Second. Together, these three wards made up the heart of the Democratic Machine. State Street, the shopping thoroughfare developed by Potter Palmer and his father-in-law, is the major thoroughfare uniting the below-river wards. State Street's First Ward portion became Palmer's shopping paradise, while the Second portion spawned Hell's Mile and Levee prostitution district.

Votes were harvested on mass by ward heelers, who made up a good chunk of that private army McDonald drew around himself after 1861. Many heelers were alcoholics. Aldermen, Chicago's new powerbrokers,

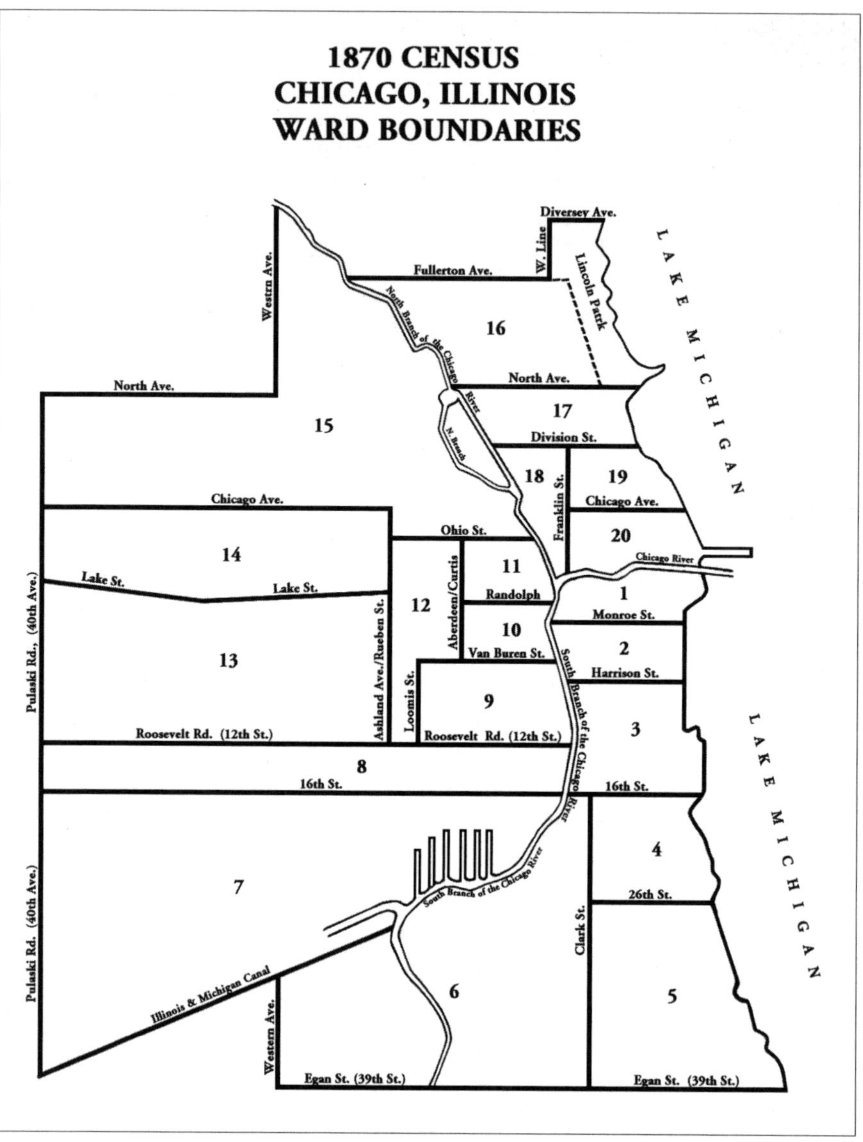

Chicago's 1870 voting wards, heart of the "Democratic Machine": McDonald's home base was the Twentieth Ward, while the "Lords of the Levee" delivered Wards 1 and 2. *alookatcook.info*.

tended to be drawn from the ranks of saloonkeepers, so saloons became clearinghouses for vote collection. Lindberg:

> *Endorsed and supported by the powerful liquor lobby and ethnic fraternal societies organized to defend the saloon trade against Prohibition and blue laws, McDonald's "ward heelers" were deployed across the city to organize the voters and seize control of the courts, the office of city hall, the bail bondsmen, the police and fire departments, the Cook County Hospital, the sheriff, and wherever else opportunity lurked to plunder the city treasury and acquire "boodle."* [11]

Ward heelers offered the carrot—men might be paid in booze to vote—while the stick came from "shoulder hitters," who were a type of marching hoodlum. As the working-class immigrant neighborhoods grew, this machine expanded. Fights broke out between competing ward heelers, who sometimes had ethnic organized crime loyalties.

A colorful interview with one of these ward heelers, under the identity of "Farmer Jones," is given by W.T. Stead in his *If Christ Came to Chicago*. Farmer Jones made money rounding up Italians to vote Democrat. To accomplish this, he exploited a child. Farmer Jones would send in a little Italian girl, about eight years old, to canvass under the nose of the *mafioso*, otherwise "he could never have done anything":

> *"Well," said he* [Farmer Jones], *as he lit another cigarette, "two years ago I noticed that a friend of mine who lives down the block had a bright little girl who was beginning to go to the public school. He was an Italian, and a very fine man, although he could not speak much English. I kept my eye on that little girl, and whenever I went to see her father I always took her a pound of candies, or a toy tortoise, or a snake, or anything of that kind, even if to do so I had to borrow a quarter. So I quite got hold of the little girl; she thinks I am her best friend in the world, and she will go anywhere with me, and do anything I want. When the elections come round I just go to her with a bag of candies, and we go canvassing together. She can speak both Italian and English; so she goes with me and translates anything I have got to say. I have got great hold over the Italians here, and it is all through that little girl."* [12]

Grooming can take a lot of forms, and it isn't necessarily done with an eye toward sexual abuse. After this story, "Farmer Jones" goes on to relate how the girl came between him a knife blade when he tried to sell votes out from under an Italian mafioso who was pitching the same wares.

From the civic administration level, the Kentucky Colony's rise to political power was based on the aldermen's control of lucrative civic contracts and plum jobs via the Board of Public Works. McDonald controlled the aldermen through gambling payouts and vote harvesting. The Colony controlled McDonald through selective enforcement of the law. If McDonald's gambling parlors or racetrack were closed, he'd be out of business. Pushing that "big red button" had consequences for the Colony too, because they'd need a boss to take McDonald's place or they'd lose control of elections. This fault line ruptured in the run-up to the Columbian Exposition in 1893.

Why did this rupture happen? The Colony made its leap from being a city power to that of an international power at this time. For example, in 1891–92, Bertha Palmer used Colony contacts in the White House and State Department to take her brand global at the courts of Europe while stumping for the Columbian Exposition. McDonald's clumsy criminal patronage system was too oafish for the diplomatic games Bertha played. Better "Chinese Walls" were needed between the public face and business end of the Colony's Chicago. History shows that these new walls were adequate until late 1909.

What did building new walls look like in 1890? Answer: *Vienna.* Twenty years before, Carter Harrison III saw the Hapsburgs' governing style and the effects of the 1873 Vienna World's Fair. Vienna's World's Fair was the last money-splurge of the Gründerzeit, a period wherein the imperial family handed economic opportunity to 1848 revolutionaries and pimps as a bribe for compliance. During the Gründerzeit, leading newspapermen and financial criminals colluded to profit from a global investment bubble. These refined Austrian games were more suited to men like bucket-shop owner William Skakel (Ethel Skakel Kennedy's great-uncle) than Mike McDonald. In 1890s Chicago, it was Vienna's vice of choice, tolerated prostitution, that would eclipse gambling and become the engine running Chicago's Democratic Machine.

However, in March 1876 Harrison III still needed "Gambler King" McDonald. Harrison broke his European sojourn to take up his congressional seat in Washington, D.C., from where he sought Chicago's mayoralty. Harrison III was mayor for four consecutive terms (eight years, 1879–87) thanks to McDonald.

Harrison was genuinely popular among the socialist-leaning masses:

> *Harrison was a man of enduring charisma, wry humor, and personal flamboyance. An oversized slouch hat and black cape were his famous trademarks. More important, he stirred the passions of the common man. It was an unbeatable combination.*[13]

Between Harrison III and his son alone, the Kentucky Colony would control Chicago for ten mayoral terms—twenty years—between 1879 and the Great War. All of this was accomplished through (1) voter fraud paired with (2) pandering to narrow ethnic interests. Before 1884, voter fraud *on behalf of Harrison* was overseen by either McDonald or his "private secretary" Joe Mackin, who was also secretary to the Cook County Democratic Central Committee.

9

BEEF AND THE SEX TRADE

The bosses behind the "bosses" of late nineteenth-century Chicago were the Kentucky Colony, and their golden son, Mayor Charter Harrison III, ruled over the city by keeping his gangsters on the civic payroll.

The Kentucky Colony was never just the Louisville families, though. New blood was allowed entry, for instance, the family of W.S. Bryan, the cousin of politician William Jennings Bryan. One had to control a useful resource to gain entry to this charmed circle. In Chicago's history, no resource was more useful than the railways, but it was the meatpackers, not the rail magnates, who won control of the railways.

How did this strange situation come about? Monopsony: a consortium of meatpackers led by Philip Danforth Armour brought so much freight custom to the railways that the packers could dictate freight prices and routes. The railways cannibalized themselves chasing the beef business. This battle had bizarre consequences: the career of Abraham Lincoln was one, as was Chicago's massive red-light district known as Hell's Mile, of which the Levee was an elite section.

Prior to the Civil War, Chicago's railway battle had four combatants: (1) New York's economic winners, the robber barons; (2) Southern railway builders; (3) local rail developers and their abolitionist East Coast allies; and finally (4) the commodity middlemen on Chicago's Board of Trade. As time went on, the last two combatants had more and more in common.

Battle lines were actually drawn over a canal, the Illinois and Michigan Canal (I&M), rather than a railway. Construction of the Erie Canal (1817–25)

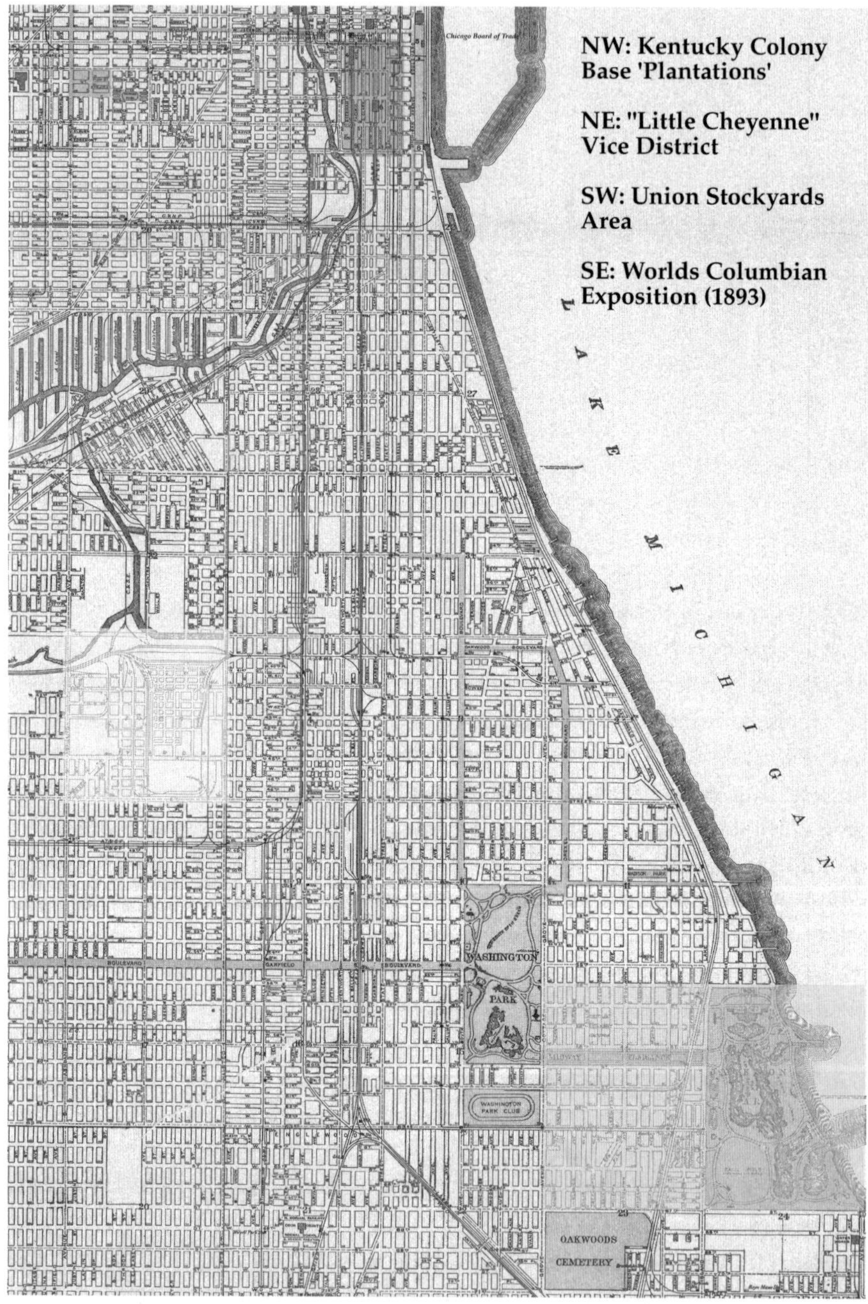

Chicago 1897/9 map showing (*clockwise from noon*) the "Little Cheyenne" district; Columbian Exposition location; Union Stockyards/"Packingtown"; the Kentucky Colony base. *University of Chicago Library.*

made it clear to New York businessmen how much power came from dictating how things are moved about. Far-sighted investors envisioned a web of canals joining New York to New Orleans. The key thread in this web was Chicago's I&M.[1]

But who would pay for the I&M Canal? Congress granted a land subsidy to finance the endeavor in 1827: $284,000 and alternating plots of land five miles deep each side of the ditch.[2] Back in Illinois, however, the mood was less optimistic. The canal project was pushed through against the wishes of the Southern-leaning south half of the state, which refused to pay taxes for it. Illinois' legislature dragged its feet until the whole undertaking was sunk when state finances collapsed in 1842.

Then I&M financing went global. Canal investors including William Ogden (a founding member of the Board of Trade)[3] devised a scheme where "foreign bondholders," specifically Barings Bank and Magniac, Jardine & Co., could buy the canal from the state for $1.6 million. Despite the cost to build it so far being $5 million, this deal went through.

From its earliest days, the Chicago Board of Trade (CBoT), a lobby for the city's business community, had a cozy relationship with both Chicago's Common Council (the mayor and aldermen) and the new owners of the I&M Canal. Thomas Richmond, of Richmond House and another founding CBoT member, continually pushed Barings for better canal maintenance. Quite often, the Board worked out a deals where taxpayers paid for canal operating expenses.[4]

Herein lies the germ of Chicago's political conflicts. The foreign bondholders hired U.S. Senator John Davis of Massachusetts to assess the canal project for them.[5] Senator Davis was a Whig and married to the sister of George Bancroft of the Bancroft treaties with Prussia.[6] The sweetheart deals enjoyed by I&M beneficiaries via Senator Davis established a culture of corruption that benefited Yankee Whigs and their offspring the Lincoln Republicans.

Who were the foreign bondholders? The Barings Bank of London was the British node of a Europe-wide banking family, the Anglo-German Barings clan, who were originally from Bremen. Magniac, Jardine & Co. were a partnership of anglicized French Huguenot brothers and a Scotsman, all three of whom profited from the Old China Trade (opium). Both firms were part of London's cosmopolitan unorthodox investor community. This international community comprised the true rulers of the British empire and had been for sixty years by the time of the firms' I&M Canal purchase.[7]

William B. Ogden as painted by George Healy in 1855. Prior to his business success, Ogden was Chicago's first mayor in 1837. *Wikimedia Commons.*

Just one year after the foreign bondholders picked up the I&M, it opened for shipping. In less than a decade, however, the importance of the canal was eclipsed by railroads. It was obvious that power now lay in controlling the railroads, so I&M investors turned their gaze accordingly.

In 1845, a group of businessmen led by William B. Ogden (from the I&M) and Jonathan Young Scammon[8] sought to develop the Galena-Chicago Union Railway. Ogden and Scammon paid for the surveying, which began in late 1846. Ogden became the railway's president.

In order to finance this Galena railway, Ogden, Scammon and other I&M investors scoured the region for capital, but interest was muted. Therefore, Ogden repeated his earlier I&M tactics. He organized with "the principle commercial men in Detroit, Buffalo, Boston, Springfield, and New York" to lobby the federal government for funds to improve Chicago's infrastructure. They set up a business convention which attracted the "leading men" of "New England, New York, Pennsylvania, New Jersey, Georgia, Florida, Kentucky and all the Western States north of the Ohio River, including Missouri and Iowa west of the Mississippi."[9]

We know that this convention had the support of abolitionist William H. Seward's camp back in New York State, because Seward's mouthpiece Horace Greeley of the *New York Tribune* as well as Thurlow Weed made a point of attending.[10] The result of this campaign was that Ogden tied Chicago's local business community to New York's radical Whigs.[11]

Ogden's radical Whig strategy was born from necessity. He and the former I&M investors were railroad underdogs, trailing the magnates of New York and the South in their race to lay Chicago's tracks. This was a bitter struggle. Even before the Civil War, the CBoT grappled with New York railwaymen over access to the East Coast and ultimately European markets. Erastus Corning's New York Central Railroad and the Erie Railroad[12] of Daniel Drew, and later James Fisk and Jay Gould, had the CBoT between their pincers. These railroads would gouge merchants through discriminatory pricing. Chicago merchants, particularly Thomas Richmond, endlessly courted Canadian transport magnates in hopes of finding a way around the robber barons.

Southern railwaymen scared Richmond and Ogden just as much. Southern magnates built railroads cheaper, controlled coveted lines serving the Mississippi and Ohio Rivers[13] and even had strong political support in Illinois' lower half. In addition, the pathetically corrupt state of Midwestern banking left Chicago commerce dependent on Southern-allied financiers for financial services.

Therefore, if Chicago men wanted to control that New York–New Orleans transportation web, their only shot was to corner the railway service between Chicago and the Northwest: Wisconsin, Minnesota, Iowa and Nebraska. To achieve this, they needed politically isolated funding from New York (Seward's radical Whigs) and they needed to limit Southern expansion—in other words, prevent further slaveholding states from being created in the Western territories. So was the Party of Lincoln born.

Abraham Lincoln was an excellent investment for Richmond and the CBoT. Lincoln should be remembered as the president who created a new railroad power in the North. Indeed, the Republican Party was first and foremost the party of these new railroad lords, and it was Lincoln's 1862 Pacific Railway Act that catapulted Chicago's underdogs to preeminence.

While Ogden's Galena railroad had prospered through the 1850s, Seward's political career floundered because of his dishonorable tactics, which alienated the Whig base. A bevy of disappointed New York City millionaires around the Cooper Union technical college sought to replace Seward with a less tarnished candidate.[14] Greeley found them one named Abraham Lincoln.

As Seward sank, rats left his ship and headed for the Midwest: William Ogden partnered with these Seward political orphans to found the Mississippi and Missouri Railroad Company (MS & MO RR), which connected Iowa to Chicago. These orphans included members of the new Republican Party and abolitionist "Barnburner" Democrats who served under Seward when he was governor of New York. Prominent MS & MO RR orphans were Azariah Cutting Flagg and John Adams Dix of the Cooper Union crowd.

MS & MO RR was supported by Elisha C. Litchfield and George Bliss, the prewar Yankee financiers of the Michigan Lake Shore Railway, which was the only non-Canadian route around Lake Erie from Chicago to New York.[15] (This Yankee pair would lose the Lake Shore Line to robber baron Vanderbilt in 1867.) Flagg and Bliss were also given executive positions on the Chicago and Rock Island Railway Company (C&RI RR), which quickly absorbed the MS & MO RR.[16] A shady duo of brokers, Henry Farnam and Dr. Thomas C. Durant (doctor of medicine), were tasked with selling securities to finance these ventures. The syndicate hired Grenville Mellen Dodge as a surveyor.

Left: Azariah Cutting Flagg was New York state comptroller twice under Governor William Seward. *Library of Congress.*

Right: John Adams Dix served as New York's secretary of state under Governor William Seward. *Library of Congress.*

Left: Lincoln's Civil War spymaster and cotton smuggler Grenville Mellen Dodge. *National Portrait Gallery, Smithsonian Institution.*

Right: Thomas C. Durant, Lincoln's most visible railway magnate and Dodge's cotton-smuggling partner. *National Archives and Records Administration.*

C&RI RR infrastructure projects were done with a carelessness that would keep the CBoT busy lobbying on their behalf. In 1857, the venture built a low wooden bridge joining two lines across the Mississippi River. This bridge was poorly designed: a ship struck it, and a legal battle commenced between the railroad operators and South-aligned Mississippi shippers,[17] during which the Chicago Board of Trade sided squarely with Durant. Durant hired Abraham Lincoln to be C&RI's representation in resulting lawsuits.

When Lincoln created his new railway power in 1862, he put Durant at the head of the Union Pacific Railway. The wisdom of this was revealed when Durant exploded the Crédit Mobilier of America, causing yet another financial scandal for President Ulysses S. Grant.

Beyond staffing his pet railways, Lincoln would roll these C&RI RR men into elite Union army positions during the Civil War: Dodge became the Union's intelligence chief and worked closely with counterfeiting expert Allan Pinkerton, while Dix became a major general and provisioner. During the war, Durant would work with spy chief Dodge to run an important syndicate smuggling cotton out of the South. (Potter Palmer just happened to make a fortune selling cotton to the Union army during that conflict.)

The most powerful faction at the CBoT supported Lincoln, and the Board even financed two regiments for the Union. Certainly there were Kentucky Colony members who sympathized with the South, but ultimately the Colony were in it for themselves. Carter Harrison IV recollected (after the war) that his clique viewed Lincoln as a "martyr"[18]—maybe they did; their neighbor Arabut Ludlow certainly had reason to. This elite consensus was broadcast by Joseph Medill, whose newspaper put the Board's presidential candidate on the nation's political map.

Medill was a Canadian abolitionist who in 1855 moved to Chicago on the advice of Horace Greeley.[19] Greeley told Medill to partner with Dr. Charles Ray of Galena, Illinois, to buy the *Chicago Tribune*.[20]

Dr. Ray was a scandal-plagued medical doctor who became a temperance activist and newspaper publisher.[21] Together, Ray and Medill made "the failing *Chicago Tribune* into one of the most powerful antislavery newspapers in the country, giving unwavering editorial support to Abraham Lincoln throughout his political career."[22] Lincoln was widely seen as Seward's political successor. In 1874, Marshall Field lent Medill the money to buy the *Tribune* outright.

Lincoln's early death left Chicago's home-grown railwaymen to contend with other Yankee competitors. For example, the 1867–89 period saw the Vanderbilts grab an astounding amount of Chicago's track, to the point where they dominated the meatpacking industry through their control of the Union Stockyards, the hub where trains brought cattle to slaughter. The Vanderbilts' hold was broken only by the power of the Beef Trust, a monopoly of CBoT meatpackers led by Philip Danforth Armour.

At least part of the Kentucky Colony's political longevity can be attributed to their good relations with peers like Philip Danforth Armour. (Arabut Ludlow himself made zero-interest loans to Armour & Co. and invested $10,000 of his estate in the firm.)[23] Armour's Beef Trust managed to escape most public scrutiny and laughed off government regulation. Writing in 1905, journalist Charles Edward Russell described the Beef Trust in this way:

> *In the free republic of the United States of America is a power greater than the government, greater than the courts or judges, greater than legislature, superior to and independent of all authority of state or nation.*[24]

This was no exaggeration. By 1905, Armour's trust controlled global meat markets; it dominated the U.S. trade in fertilizers, including the precious phosphate mines near Sarasota, Florida; and it owned a bevy of steam and electric railroads, "the entire trolley-car service in several cities" and a glorious real estate portfolio. The Beef Trust also owned politicians, legislators and congressmen. The Trust was able to ignore both the Senate's antitrust *Vest Committee Report* (1889); the U.S. Supreme Court's ruling to dissolve the Trust and a slew of state regulations throughout the Middle West.

New York native Philip Danforth Armour organized the Beef Trust, and his son Jonathan Ogden Armour would control it after 1905. *National Portrait Gallery, Smithsonian Institution.*

The Beef Trust was not a typical trust; it existed in the coordinated efforts of four separate companies owned by Armour and the other Packingtown magnates: Gustavus F. Swift, Nelson Morris and George H. Hammond. The Beef Trust wasn't really a meat trust, either. It was a railroad trust.

Lincoln's railways grew east–west to meet cattle drives originating in Texas. Therefore, railroads were built where the cattlemen needed them, which gave the beef market huge power over the railways. But where did the cattlemen need the trains? Wherever their army of cowboys would drive the cattle.

Cowboys, a diverse, impulsive and crime-prone group of men, would drive cattle only through towns that tolerated prostitution.[25] The sex trade stabilized the cattle drives for the railroads and meatpackers while at the same time provided illegal tax revenue for policing cowboys. This tolerated vice system was first set up along the cattle trails by Chicago cattleman Joseph McCoy in Abilene, Kansas.[26] Tolerated prostitution *always* corrupts local politics, and violent cowboys were treated leniently by judges at the behest of prominent businessmen.[27] The beef business became the engine that propelled both the sex trade and government corruption.

Just as with Florida's phosphate mines and railroads, the cattle trade enjoyed British investment after the Civil War. For example, the Ten in Texas (XIT) ranch, which used the Great Western Trail, was owned by Marshall Field's first employer, Chicagoan John Villiers Farwell, and a bevy of British aristocrats like the Marquis of Tweeddale and the Earl of Aberdeen. This was the largest cattle ranch in the world.

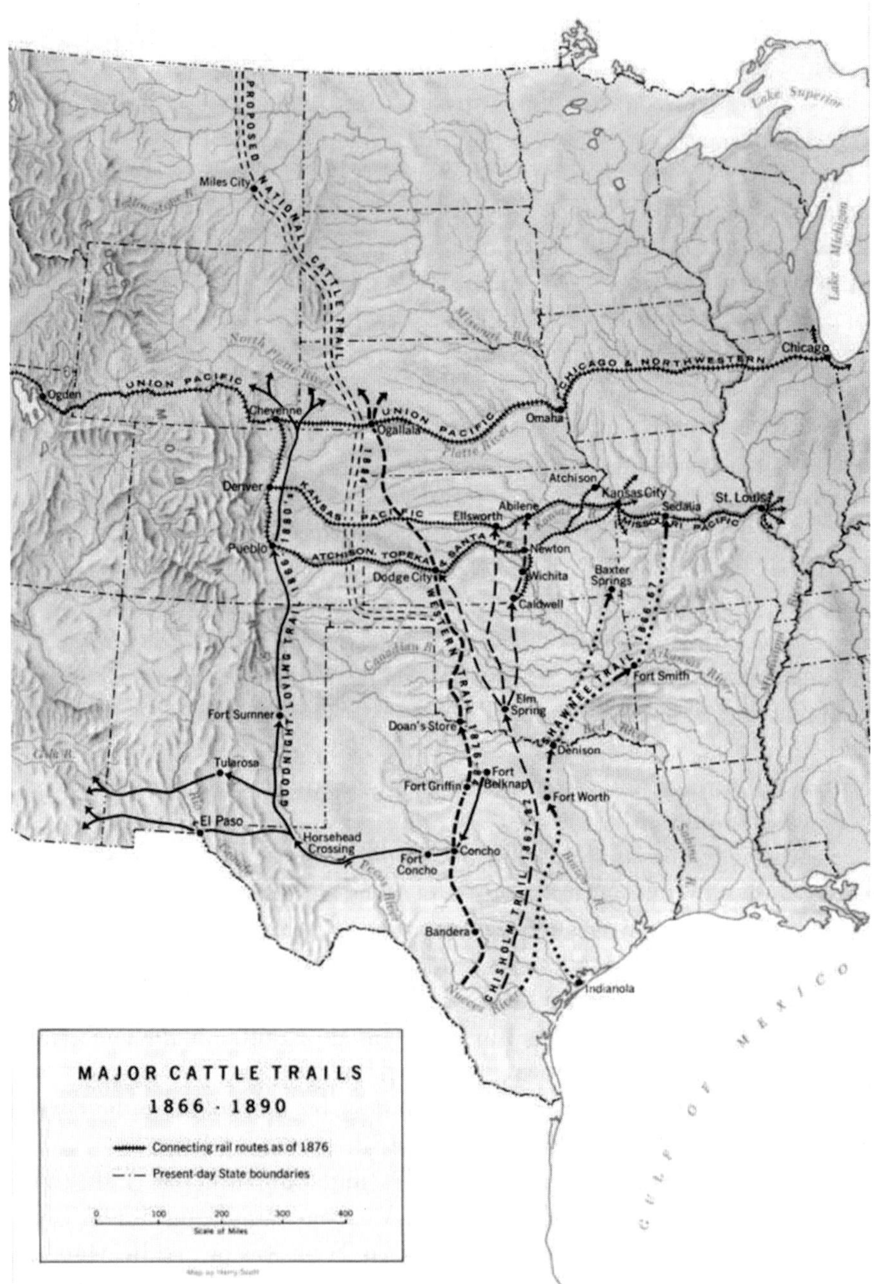

As the 1870s progressed, cattle trails were pushed westward and the Lincoln railroads stretched to meet them. *National Parks Service.*

Cattle trail vice reinforced problems in the ultimate railhead town, Chicago. Both sex and meat were traded for cash, not credit. A city with a big meat market needed financial institutions that were able to meet huge cyclical demands for cash. Gamblers, counterfeiters and other con artists like cash, too. The consequence of this banking/vice/beef synergy was that the meat trade bolstered Chicago's sex tourism. For example, poorly planned office buildings, not unlike those thrown up by H.H. Honoré and Potter Palmer around State Street after the 1871 fire,[28] were typically converted into bordellos that catered to traveling businessmen.[29] These synergies are why the Chicago Board of Trade tolerated prostitution south of the central business district. Hell's Mile grew up between the Palmer House Hotel and the Union Stockyards.

Rail magnates did not passively accept beef industry power. By the 1880s, Vanderbilt domination of the Union Stockyards had convinced Beef Trust companies to diversify butchering outside of Chicago. Ultimately, the top meatpackers were better organized and used their monopsony to tame the Vanderbilts.

The Beef Trust put their packinghouse competitors out of business by forcing the railroads to subsidize Beef Trust products with "rebates." Railroads actually paid the Beef Trust to pull Trust-owned refrigerated cars. Naturally, competitors couldn't get their meat out east so cheaply and were eventually driven out of business. The Trust was in operation by 1889, and by 1900 it owned almost every American meatpacking concern. (By 1905, J. Ogden Armour controlled the Trust due to the deaths of founding members and buyouts.)[30] Between father and son, the Armours had turned the CBoT's discriminatory pricing troubles with the railways upside down.

Meat wasn't the only product that relied on refrigerated cars, and the Trust branched out into every conceivable foodstuff. It was particularly influential in the nation's fruit industry, including that around Sarasota, Florida, where both the Armours and Bertha Palmer made heavy investments. As Armour gouged the railways, these costs were passed on to lesser producers and consumers. Armour levied his own taxes on the nation.[31]

If readers have heard of Armour's empire, it is probably in relation to Upton Sinclair's novel *The Jungle*, which describes horrific working and living conditions around Chicago's stockyards. Armour was a huge employer of those immigrant hordes that poured into Chicago and fed the Colony via McDonald's "Democratic Machine." To this end, Armour had a lot in common with Lincoln's abolitionist supporters. At the war's conclusion, Armour made a concerted effort to recruit "exodusters," freed slaves, and encouraged Chicago's elite to subsidize them. The new Black recruits from the South undermined Armour's employees' attempts to improve their working conditions. The horrific "jungle" came as a result of abolition, exactly the situation both Yankee Know Nothings and Copperhead working men feared. The greed of Chicago's plutocracy stoked their socialism problem.

While Armour worked to import fodder for McDonald's machine, he also funded the Republican Party. Charles G. Dawes, Republican President McKinley's comptroller of the currency, retired to lead the Beef Trust's Central Trust Company. Central Trust stockholder Frank O. Lowden[32] served Illinois as a Republican congressman, governor and presidential nominee. (His wife was George Pullman's daughter.)[33] Stockholder Graeme Stewart was the 1904 Republican candidate for mayor of Chicago and a Teddy Roosevelt supporter.[34] Republican Congressman William Lorimer of Illinois, an English immigrant known as the "blond boss," was an ardent defender of Beef Trust interests.[35]

The lines between political parties in Chicago were never very clear. Take, for instance, the scandal of the Whiskey Ring (1871–76). President Grant's secretary Orville Babcock was "deeply implicated" in this industrial scale tax dodge, as were Mike McDonald and Anton Hesing, the Republican publisher of the *Illinois Staats Zeitung*.[36] Hesing even did jail time for the swindle. McDonald didn't do time, but he did do a lot of campaigning for President Grant in 1872.[37] The leaders of Chicago's underworld were the leaders of the city's political parties on both sides of the aisle.

Brigadier General Charles Gates Dawes was a spokesman for Morgan banking interests. He would later be known for his ill-advised World War I "reparations" plan. *National Archives and Records Administration/ Wikimedia Commons.*

Inter-party alliances were kinship based too. In 1874, President Grant's son married Bertha Palmer's sister Ida Marie Honoré, uniting two of the Midwest's great "opposing" political families. According to Bertha's heirs, the president valued the Democrat socialite as part of his receiving entourage.[38]

While the newspapers on both Republican and Democratic sides made a show of animosity, the reality is that Marshall Field, Philip Armour and others were friendly enough with Carter

Bertha Palmer, painted for the Columbian Exposition by A. Zorn. Bertha's fashion mimics Elisabeth of Austria's style, and she even adopted the empress's nickname "Cissie." *Art Institute of Chicago.*

Harrison III to extol him as a "great mayor, a civic leader, and a cordial old friend" after his 1893 assassination. Joseph Medill, the anti-Harrison *Chicago Tribune* editor, was asked to be an honorary pallbearer.[39]

Medill's political career in Chicago deserves scrutiny given what we know about Lincoln's supporters in Monroe, Wisconsin. Carter Harrison III supported Medill's mayorship,[40] and Medill's abrupt resignation in August 1873 allowed McDonald to install a United States Express Company executive in his stead, one Harvey Doolittle Colvin (1873–76). The U.S. Express was central to Latta's counterfeiting enterprise.

Mayor Colvin enabled Republican boss Anton Hesing's and Democrat McDonald's graft systems to balloon. (Marshall Field bought the *Tribune* for Medill as opposition during the Colvin mayoralty.)[41] When McDonald installed Democrat DeWitt Clinton Cregier as mayor in 1889, Marshall Field provided Cregier's mayoral bond.[42] The same names were behind both parties.

Above the muck of politics, other relationships flourished. Marshall Field befriended railway sleeper-car magnate George Mortimer Pullman as well as P.D. Armour. They were known as the "trinity of Chicago business" and would walk to work together because they all lived on "Prairie Avenue," until the stink of Armour's stockyards drove everybody north to Palmer's "Gold Coast."[43]

The glitz of Chicago's millionaires was never far from the slime of the Levee. Chicago's elite families, those Mike McDonald's crime syndicate could not touch, were the leaders of the Republican and Democrat Parties alike. They profited from rampant vice. They triumphed on the Board of Trade. Their shining star was Potter Palmer's wife, Bertha Honoré Palmer, and her Palmer House Hotel.

10

THE PALMER HOUSE HOTEL

By the 1880s, the Palmer House Hotel was the nexus of Chicago's political and sex trade underworlds. Ten years prior, Potter Palmer had gifted the building to his bride, Bertha Honoré. The money came from Potter's wartime cotton trade, when Lincoln's spy chief Grenville M. Dodge ran a cotton smuggling ring out of the South.[1]

Bertha's hotel justly earned a reputation for ostentatious display. For example, silver dollar coins were set into its barbershop tiles. Hotel patrons included actresses like Sarah Bernhardt and Helena Modjeska,[2] who were considered courtesans and excluded by upper-class hotels. Bertha's establishment became a staple of Chicago's sex tourism scene:

> *A scouring scrub at the Palmer House Hotel following a roaring night in the Levee was considered one of the grandest luxuries the nation afforded, and visiting dignitaries often availed themselves of this delightful, if enervating, experience.*[3]

Information on the doings of visiting dignitaries is a valuable sex-trade byproduct, and Potter Palmer watched hotel patrons from his glass-walled office in Bertha's lobby.[4] The Levee was the elite section of Chicago's prostitution district. After 1898, the star Levee bordello was the Everleigh Club, where Medill's *Chicago Tribune* reporters were given run of the house.[5]

Beyond prostitution, Bertha's hotel became a proofing ground for McDonald's crime world subordinates. These "Lords of the Levee" controlled the Democratic Machine and taxed all madams. McDonald's

The famous Palmer House Hotel in Chicago, photo taken between 1900 and 1910. *Library of Congress.*

right-hand man, Joseph Mackin, took up permanent residence at the Palmer House Hotel.[6] Mackin ran the Cook County (Chicago) Democratic Central Committee and as a young politico ran in the same circles as William Jennings Bryan.[7]

John Coughlin, Levee Lord after the Columbian Exposition, got his start at the Palmer House, where he met all the right people:

> *A year later* [around 1876] [John "Bathhouse"] *Coughlin got a job in the Palmer House baths, reaching the status of head rubber in a few months. Here came the big politicians and businessmen, the congressmen and senators traveling through from Washington, and, on rare occasions, a personage as distinguished as Marshall Field. Coughlin was a favorite with these men; he learned their whims and how to please them.*[8]

The brains behind Coughlin, Michael "Hinky Dink" Kenna, got his start working for Joseph Medill at the *Chicago Tribune*.[9]

"Levee Lord" John "Bathhouse" Coughlin was one-half of the duo who ran Chicago's post-1893 top vice industry: prostitution. *Author's collection.*

Left: "Levee Lord" Michael "Hinky Dink" Kenna was the brains behind Bathhouse John's charm. Kenna got the monicker "Hinky Dink" from his boss Joseph Medill. *Wikipedia*.

Right: John "Mushmouth" Johnson, Chicago's Black vice lord. His role was to oversee the Black vote. *Wikipedia*.

Another Palmer House Turkish Bath graduate was Freddie Train, a leading brothel owner in the Levee. Train was a stalwart supporter of Coughlin's career overseeing vote-harvesting for Chicago's Democratic Party.

Chicago's first Black vice lord was John "Mushmouth" Johnson, so named for his foul language.[10] Johnson got his start as a waiter at the Palmer House, which, like the Everleigh Club,[11] gave preference to Blacks for service positions.[12] It was commonly held that Johnson's mother was a nurse for Abraham Lincoln's wife.[13] After serving at the Palmer House, Johnson opened a saloon and gambling house on Palmer's State Street:

> *Calling himself "the Negro Gambling King of Chicago", Mushmouth Johnson cultivated the usual arrangement with Bathhouse John and Hinky Dink, delivering votes and protection payments in exchange for legal immunity and the title "Negro political boss" in their First Ward.*[14]

As the Black population of Chicago grew, shepherding their votes became important. Chicago's employers particularly sought them to break strikes.[15]

Both the Armour family and Marshall Field were proactive organizing Chicago's Black community.[16] Meatpackers kept wages low by inciting racial animosity between stockyard workers through conspicuous charitable giving to Black causes.[17]

As the 1900s rolled around, Palmer House graduate George Little became a money collector for Hinky Dink and Bathhouse. Little had worked in the stables at the Palmer House Hotel and by 1909 was the "Levee Czar."[18]

Besides shaking down bordellos, Little was also a boxing promoter. One of his talents was Jack Johnston, a Black boxer who liked White women and who would have his own slave-trading troubles.[19] It was the 1913 trial of Jack Johnston for violating the Mann Act that exploded Chicago's White-slaving problem into Midwestern newspapers. Parents pulled their daughters from jobs in department stores like Marshall Field's when these stores' role as feeder institutions for White slavery (sex trafficking) was revealed.[20] (Marshall Field's lingerie department was where Everleigh sisters let their "choicest girls" shop.)[21]

Jack Johnson (*center*) with his "Levee Czar" manager George Little. Although pardoned by President Trump in 2018, it would be remarkable if Johnson wasn't working as an enforcer for Little. *Author's collection.*

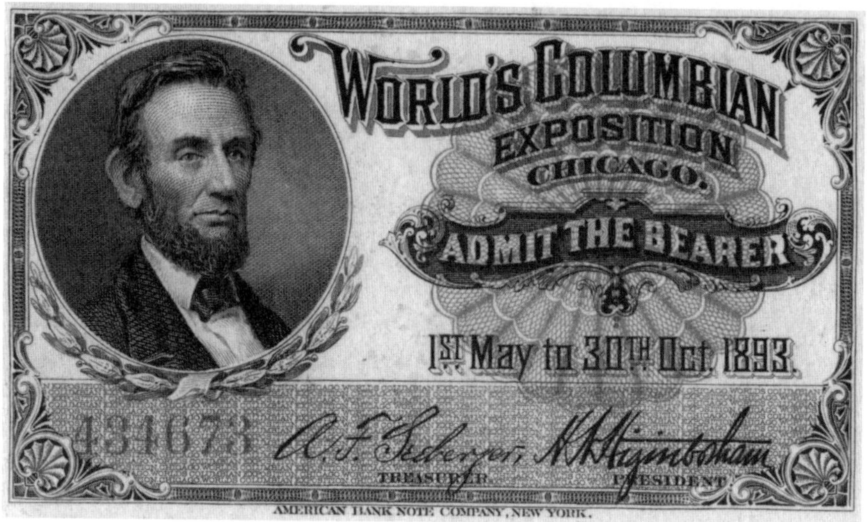

A ticket to Chicago's 1893 Columbian Exposition. Like the Vienna World's Fair of 1873, Chicago's fair coincided with the start of a major regional economic depression. *Author's collection.*

A man named Alphonse Caponi got his start as a bodyguard for Big Jim Colosimo, a Levee bordello operator under Coughlin.[22] Chicago's infamous Prohibition-era mafioso gained power through the Palmer House system as that system refocused on prostitution after the Columbian Exposition of 1893.

The Columbian Exposition was the Kentucky Colony's crowning achievement in both national politics and local organized crime. They'd swept away gambling king McDonald and weaned his vote-harvesting racket onto prostitution money with the help of new Hapsburg criminals. Harrison III reinstated himself as mayor for the event. Coughlin was allegedly appointed to the exposition's welcoming committee.[23] Chicago's sex trade geared up for more patronage than ever before.[24]

The amount of money that poured into the Levee between 1890 and 1900 was staggering,[25] as the picture from the *Chicago Tribune* on the next page illustrates.

By the 1890s, Chicago's red-light district stretched down State Street for almost a mile and was a few blocks thick either side.[26] There were bordellos that specialized in the sale of Japanese, Chinese, French and Italian people besides native-born Americans and the various nationalities of the Austrian and Russian empires. (Mushmouth Johnson controlled the Chinese, too.)[27] The advertising synergies between Hell's Mile and the spectacle of the Midway Plaisance was not lost on men like Coughlin and his sponsors.

THE CHICAGO TRIBUNE: SUNDAY, JULY 7, 1901.

TWO PICTURES SHOWING STRIKING CHANGES IN LEVEE DISTRICT DURING TEN YEARS.

THE NEW

THE OLD

RETIREMENT IS A PUZZLE.

BUSINESS-MEN FAIL TO FIX AN AGE LIMIT.

he exercises only a general supervision. In general a man should retire when business ceases to be of interest to him. Then he should devote much of his time to public affairs.

As a Night Clerk Sees It.

JAMES FAGIN, Night Clerk Jackson Hotel—Quit? I've never considered it. My only thoughts are of keeping on. I'm past 60

WOMAN A RIGHT ON LEVEE

DENVER JURIST APPLIES LATE RULING TO CHICAGO.

Chicago Tribune, July 7, 1901: photograph shows how investment poured into the Levee from the beginning of exposition planning 1891 (RHS) to 1900 (LHS).

The Columbian Exposition's lowbrow entertainments along the Plaisance had aesthetic echoes from the Levee, including a preoccupation with orientalist fantasy and Islamic sex-slavery. The spirit of this entertainment was captured by the "*danse du ventre*" or belly dancing controversy.

Along the Midway's Cairo Street, dubious performers presented the "hoochie coochie" to American audiences in a way that made belly dancing synonymous with prostitution. Sol Bloom, later U.S. congressman and Franklin Delano Roosevelt's foreign policy hawk, was responsible for producing the dances. Complaints and media coverage triggered an inquiry from Isabella Beecher Hooker, a member of the exposition's Board of Lady Managers. Hooker and the board's president, Bertha Palmer, were mutually hostile.[28] Bertha wanted to promote the dancers further via a high-society party, but Hooker and others put the kibosh on mingling. One Mrs. Barker opined:

> *I shall most certainly oppose inviting the women who perform at the theaters there to meet, socially, the members of this board. They are, many of them, not representatives of foreign nations, but women of Chicago, chosen to act these disgusting parts.... I consider it our duty rather than to entertain these people to enter a protest against them and demand that the places where they perform should be closed.*[29]

This "Egyptian dancing girl" from the Columbian Exposition was not the storied "Little Egypt" but would have performed a similar act. *Library of Congress.*

Historian Katherine Vecchio identifies Mrs. Barker's assessment as "accurate"[30] and cites the case of a twelve-year-old Swedish girl who was hired as one of these dancers. Immigrant girls from Sweden, Norway, Germany and Ireland were particularly vulnerable to sex trade recruiters.[31]

Why orientalism? The White Slave Trade, which supplied many of Chicago's prostitutes,[32] was organized out of Austria-Hungary and had large-volume end terminals in Argentina and the Ottoman Empire. The fate of these people in Islamic lands was seeping into Europe's political consciousness. Traveler Samuel Cohen describes what he saw in Istanbul:

> *The inmates of the brothel are seated on low stools or on boxes or on low couches with almost nothing on in the way of clothes. Their faces are painted and powdered, but the haggard look in their eyes cannot be hidden. In almost every case, each prostitute sits in a small compartment not more than 20 to 24 inches wide with a wire netting in front facing the street. Some few have small windows.... They permit the girls to call out to the passers by. In every house the "Madame" sits near the door or close at hand to watch over the inmates. The whole scene is revolting.*[33]

Imagine Archduke Franz Ferdinand's surprise when on his visit to the Midway Plaisance's World's Congress of Beauty he saw the following:

> *The first pavilion is dedicated to the fair sex and titled "The 40 most beautiful ladies of all nations". The rush to this much promising building is quite considerable and thus we too took tickets to visit this gallery of living beauties. In small cage-like boxes on a stage sat, were lying, or stood women dressed in national costumes representing the different countries whose names were written in large letters below the sections. Here were the Swedish woman next to the fiery eyed Andalusian, the Turk next to the Chinese, the German next to the Japanese etc. to be seen. I could not refrain in the first moment to laugh out loudly as the arrangement of the cages gave the impression of a sit venia verbo—Menagerie.... While not all the ladies, and namely not "Austria" and "Croatia", might be counted among the most beautiful of the world, nevertheless some had remarkably pretty faces whose owners certainly merited a better fate.*
>
> *The Greek woman, sitting in the dress of beautiful Helen and in full awareness of her Greek profile sat on an ancient pedestal, was recognized as being a former flower girl from Freudenau. Her answers to our questions were true Viennese and filled with the desire of the girl to*

40 LADIES FROM 40 NATIONS
WORLD'S CONGRESS OF
OF BEAUTY
DRESS AND COSTUME CO

This "Congress of Beauty" building is where Emperor Franz Joseph's heir apparent saw his fellow countryfolk on display. *Library of Congress.*

These are promotional photos of the women "in small cage-like boxes" whom the Archduke Franz Ferdinand felt "merited a better fate." *Smithsonian Institution.*

> *return soon to her home. Another lady was also from Vienna where she had acted the year before as a campaign serving girl in the music and theater exposition. The Turkish girl, who lay with multiple colleagues in an improvised harem on bulging cushions and whose rich costume and the flashy diadem completed the illusion, seemed to have seen the light of the world in England. The visible joy that the Viennese girls had seeing a compatriot moved me much.*[34]

The 1893 Rand McNally map on the following page shows how easy it was for patrons to take the elevated railroad straight to the Levee from the World's Congress of Beauty building.

The Columbian Exposition's entertainments also birthed the career of Florenz Ziegfeld of the Ziegfeld Follies. Flo's father, Dr. Florence Ziegfeld, ran a music school in the Central Music Hall, which was a favorite venue for Democratic Party conventions. Dr. Ziegfeld's musical soirees were patronized by a select group, including Bertha Palmer and her husband.[35]

While not widely appreciated in contemporary musical circles, Dr. Ziegfeld made a name for himself as a facilitator on behalf of Patrick Sarsfield Gilmore, the U.S. military's "bandmaster general." Gilmore needed talent for the 1872 Boston Peace Jubilee,[36] and Dr. Ziegfeld used his relationship with Chancellor Bismark and Johann Strauss II to force participation from the Royal Prussian Kaiser Franz Grenadier Band and the famous Viennese composer.

Why would a Chicago immigrant like Dr. Ziegfeld have connections with German Europe's power elite? Biographers are silent. We do know, however, that Dr. Ziegfeld opened a new theater, the Trocadero Theater on State Street, especially to cater to the Columbian Exposition crowd.

Austro-Hungarian police identified traveling musical acts as one of the primary vectors for White slaving.[37] Dr. Ziegfeld was able to muster over two hundred such acts in a few weeks for the Trocadero.[38] His son, Flo Ziegfeld, contributed by promoting German strongman Eugene Sandow to audiences along Hell's Mile.

This portrait of Dr. Florence Ziegfeld comes from his self-published magazine, *The Philharmonic* (January 1901).

Flo Ziegfeld would go on to produce the Ziegfeld Follies in New York City and hire

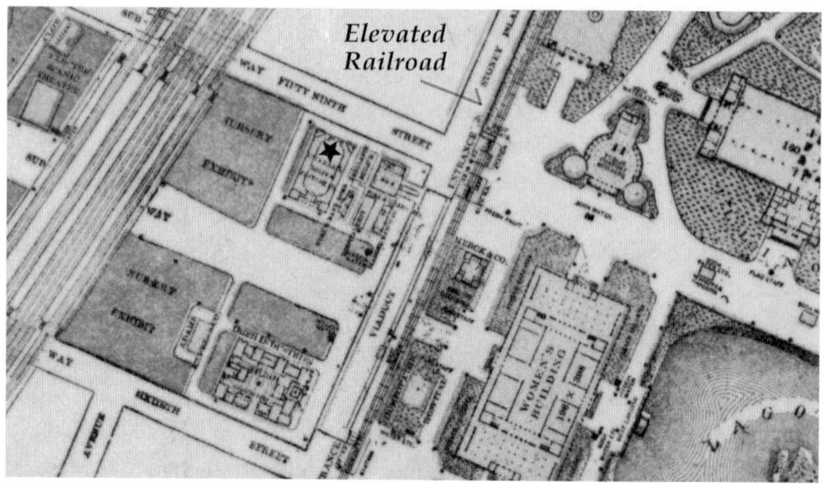

Section of 1893 souvenir map showing the "Congress of Beauty Building" (black star) at the entrance to the exposition, near the elevated rail station. *Library of Congress.*

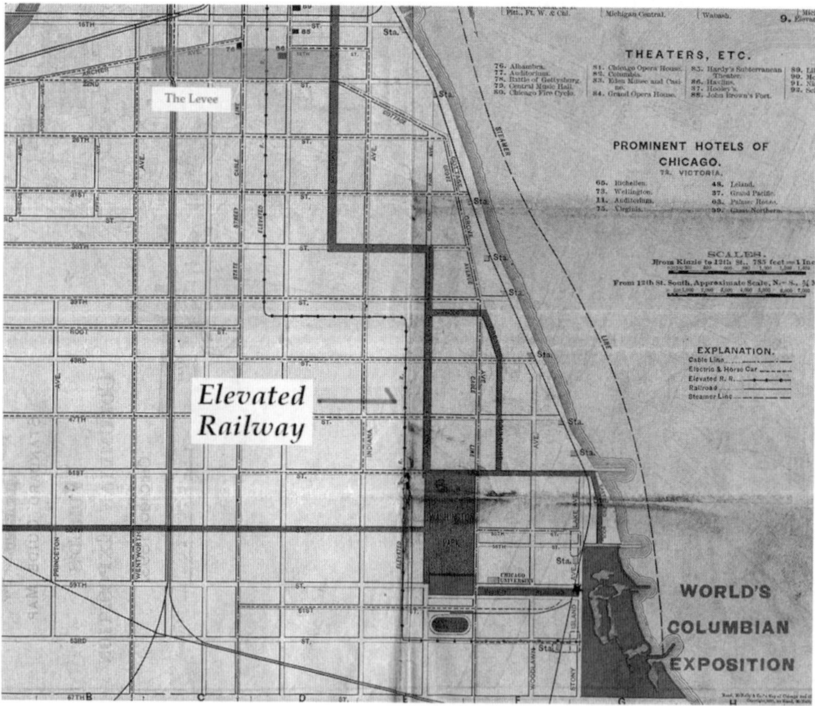

Section of 1893 Chicago World's Fair map showing Levee district in relation to the Columbian Exposition and the elevated rail line. (Beauty Congress starred.) *Tennessee State Library.*

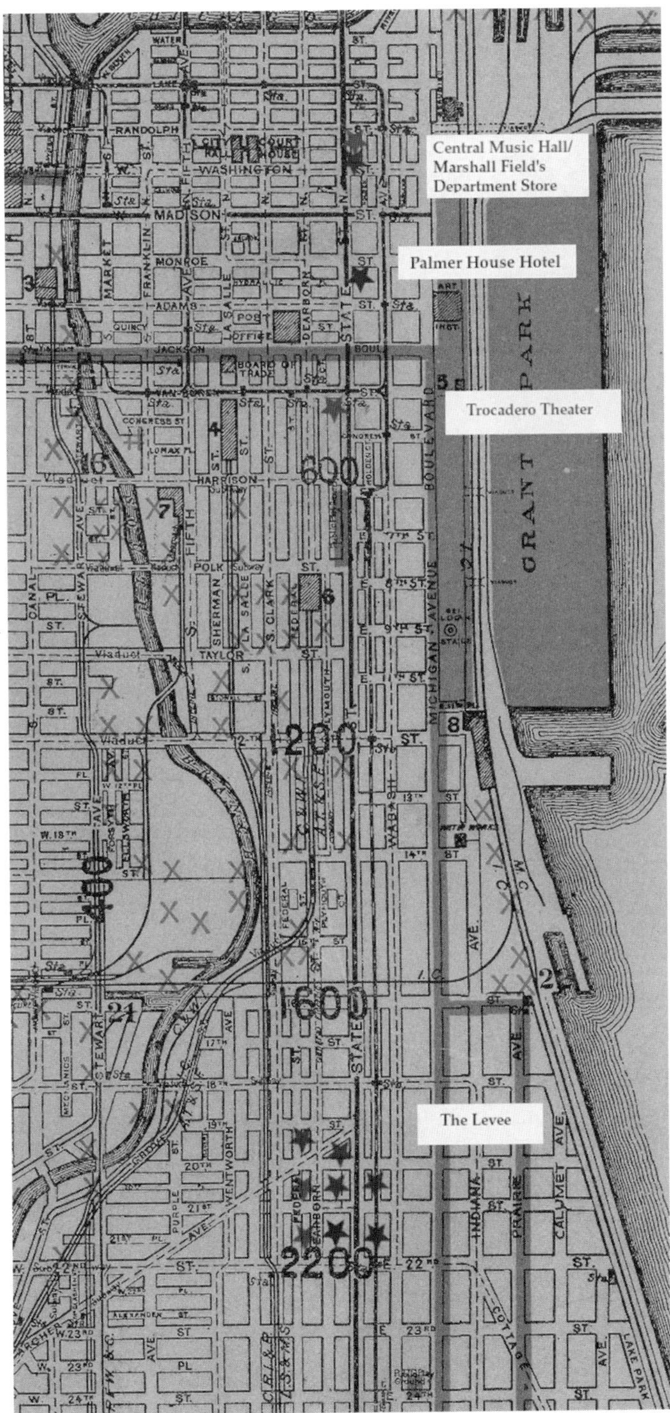

Section of 1913 Rand, McNally Chicago map showing Ziegfeld's Central Music Hall school and his Trocadero Theater in relation to other city power centers. *Wikipedia/University of Chicago.*

photographer Alfred Cheney Johnston. Ziegfeld's provocative shows displayed young women and even children like fourteen-year-old Doris Eaton. Johnson would also take nude pictures of them. Some of these pictures were kept for a secret collection that wouldn't emerge until the 1970s.[39]

The Columbian Exposition did offer more sophisticated entertainments than the Plaisance. For example, the Congress of Religions played an important role ushering in the New Age movement.

The exposition staged a number of events portraying a selection of world religions in a universalist light. Readers will remember that Universalism was the faith of Monroe's Bonelatta-era elite. Universalism teaches that all religions share the same truth, and conferences were held extolling this message. One of the conference stars was Swami Vivekananda.

Vivekananda portrayed "Hinduism" from a universalist perspective. In reality, Hinduism is not a monolithic religion, nor is India free of religious intolerance. Some people prefer the name *Sanatana dharma* to refer to the multiplicity of beliefs found on the Indian peninsula. These beliefs are highly varied, and some are even atheistic.[40]

Vivekananda's interpretation of Hinduism was heavily colored by British interests.[41] William Hastie, principal of an East India Company–founded school in Calcutta,[42] helped introduce Vivekananda to his guru Sri Ramakrishna, whose message Vivekananda broadcast in the West. Prior to Hastie's introduction, Vivekananda had already been steeped in Universalism and Western Esotericism via the teachings of Ram Mohan Roy, an assistant to a Company land-tax collector.[43] After having amassed a considerable fortune from British East India Company connections,[44] Ram Mohan Roy agitated for European-style humanist education[45] on the subcontinent alongside Company operatives.

Vivekananda's central tenet, that man can achieve godhood through knowledge, is also a core belief of Hermeticism as described in the *Pymander* text.[46] Sadly there is little scholarship examining the relationship between

Opposite: Eugene Sandow (1894) was recruited to play the Columbian Exposition by sex show entrepreneur Florenz Ziegfeld Jr., Dr. Ziegfeld's son. *Library of Congress.*

Above, left: Florenz Ziegfeld Jr. knowingly recruited Doris Eaton at fourteen years old for his organization. See Doris Eaton, *The Days We Danced* (Marquand Books, 2003), 64. *Wikipedia.*

Above, right: Ziegfeld Girl "Phyllis" in a harem-inspired costume by Lucy Duff Gordon. Orientalism was a mainstay aesthetic for both Chicago's Levee and Ziegfeld Jr.'s New York City chorus line. *Lucile, Ltd./Hearst.*

Hermeticism and *Sanatana dharma*.[47] Hermeticism is based on Greco-Egyptian magical writings. Jakob Böhme, whose philosophy inspired Universalism, has been described as a hermeticist, as have been some Renaissance humanists.[48]

Vivekananda's heady marriage of occult, hermetic and oriental culture[49] paved the way for New Age philosophical trends in the United States like Transcendental Meditation and Krishna Consciousness (Hare Krishna).[50] The Chicago Institute of Art, which enjoyed Bertha Palmer's financial support, calls Vivekananda a "key figure in the introduction of Vedanta and Yoga to the West."[51]

Coughlin's Levee would also board the hermetic bandwagon. This is not anomalous, as sex slavery and the occult have ancient links. Prior to the nineteenth century, hermetically inspired books like the *Picatrix* usually came to Europe from the Ottoman Empire in conjunction with the European slave trade.[52] These books appealed to people who had difficulty relating to others and who sought secret paths to control social superiors.[53]

Above, left: Advertisement from the *Chicago Tribune*, November 26, 1893. Both Swami Vivekanada and the Ziegfelds used the Columbian Exposition to spread their respective messages.

Above, right: A signed photograph of Swami Vivekanada, born Narendra Nath Datta to a wealthy family in Calcutta, British India, in 1863. *Wikimedia Commons.*

Opposite: Portrait of Ada Everleigh, taken around 1898, shortly before Christopher Columbus Crabb's bordello business was sold to her and sister Minna. *Douglas County Historical Society (Nebraska).*

The Levee's hermetic subculture was evidenced at the Everleigh Club bordello. Previously run by Lizzie Allen (Ellen Williams),[54] this bordello was sold to the Nebraskan Everleigh sisters in the wake of the Columbian Exposition.

Lizzie Allen's place suffered from a serial killer problem when Coughlin assumed control of Chicago's vice world in 1891.[55] Englishman Christopher Columbus Crabb ran women with Lizzie and a series other madams who died under suspicious circumstances, while Crabb always inherited their property. In 1899, Crabb retired from Lizzie's address (2131 Dearborn Street), and the business (not necessarily the property) was sold to Ada and Minna Everleigh.[56]

Why Nebraskan madams? The Everleigh sisters enjoyed some sort of patronage from the organizers of the 1898 Trans-Mississippi Exposition in

Omaha,[57] which was led by Gurdon Wallace Wattles (an early Hollywood investor) and promoted by William Jennings Bryan.[58] Bryan's cousin was a Kentucky Colony stalwart. Soon Coughlin would honor the sisters as perennial queens of his notorious First Ward Ball.[59]

Information is a valuable byproduct of the sex trade, and the sisters targeted visiting dignitaries with hermetically inspired sex amusements.[60] For example, the sisters employed blood- and sex-magic rituals to entertain Crown Prince Henry of Prussia in 1902:

Above: Everleigh Club "Moorish" room before forced closure in 1911. Moorish pirates were voracious slavers; premiums were placed on Europeans for sexual exploitation. *University of Chicago Library.*

Opposite: Everleigh Club "Mosque" room. Levee chic featured an "Orientalist" Islamic aesthetic, echoing centuries of the European slave trade. *The University of Chicago Library.*

> *A servant wheeled a bull made entirely of cloth into the room. The girls raced toward the structure, punching its head and biting its hide, spitting white flurries of cotton. Minna* [Everleigh] *watched, nodding with approval. It was perfect, she thought. This was exactly how the infant Dionysus-Zagreus had been killed. For sound effects, a male butler bellowed each time a mouth clamped down on the bull. Then Minna pointed a finger, and servants fetched platters piled with uncooked sirloin. For ten minutes, the harlots tore into the raw strips, ripping the meat with feral bites, their faces stained with pink slashes of animal blood....*
>
> *When the platters were empty, Minna threw on the lights. She would now take their visitors for a grand tour of the Club. The harlots trooped back upstairs, changed from their fawnskins into evening gowns, pinned up their hair, wiped the blood from their cheeks. A few girls brought dignitaries*

> *to their boudoirs, eager to display other talents besides play acting Greek mythology, and hurried downstairs to join the champagne toast when their guests were satisfied.*[61]

The international reputation of that night lived on in the custom of drinking champagne from a prostitute's shoe. According to historian Karen Abbot, the Kaiser was not amused.[62] According to Bertha's heirs, her son Honoré, her husband and her brother Adrienne Honoré were in charge of entertaining the prince during his visit.[63] Did what happened in Chicago stay in Chicago? Bertha's own career with Edward VII suggests not.

Crown Prince Albert Edward first came to Chicago in 1860 when his promiscuous ways had become known to his parents.[64] His father would be dead in less than a year, having been weakened by a trip to Ireland in order to dissuade Bertie from sleeping with actresses in his military tent. While touring Chicago, Bertie was chaperoned by two Galena and Chicago Railway surveyors.

Bertie's next Chicago handler was Bertha Palmer, beginning in 1907. Bertha would provide her Biarritz home to the king for liaisons with his mistress Mrs. George (Alice) Keppel.[65] Bertha would also arrange for him a banned pornographic entertainment, Strauss's *Salome*, with its titillating "Dance of the Seven Veils."[66] When Edward died, Bertha was no longer welcome with the royal family.[67] Her contact with the king seems to have come from the "unorthodox investor" Anglo-German banker Ernest Cassel.

What sort of woman was Bertha Honoré Palmer? Not one afraid of contradiction: she would lobby for temperance or support anti-trafficking activist W.T. Stead while owning one of the most successful bars in Chicago at the notorious Palmer House.[68] All over the world, contemporary sex trade dons made a habit of subverting their critics with well-placed donations.[69]

Sources agree that Bertha Palmer's nomadic lifestyle had one constant: she hung Renoir's *Acrobats at the Cirque Fernando* in her sleeping quarters. She bought the painting while lobbying in Europe for the Columbian Exposition.

From the Chicago Institute of Art's commentary on the painting:

> *The partially visible, darkly clothed (mainly male) spectators allude to the less wholesome, nocturnal demimonde of the nineteenth-century circus in which these two young performers grew up.*[70]

The children, representations of sisters Francisca and Angelina Wartenberg, were painted to look younger than they were at the time, which was fourteen and seventeen years old, respectively. The sex trade put a premium on youth,[71] and oranges symbolized theatrical prostitution.[72] Renoir's artistic publicity would have increased the value of the girls' time. Such was Mrs. Palmer's taste in art.

Bertha Palmer's fortunes took a turn for the worse in 1910: she lost Edward VII's patronage and made an unexpected decision to relocate to Sarasota, Florida, that February.[73] A week or two earlier, on January 27, the Woman's Christian Temperance Union led a highly visible march against Chicago's sex trade,[74] while Illinois congressman James Mann's anti-trafficking act had circulated since December 6, 1909. Against his own wishes, Mayor Carter Harrison IV was forced to close the Levee, including the Everleigh Club. In addition, Chicagoans were asking questions about a missing $50,000 for which Bertha was responsible as a result the Columbian Exposition.[75] Next stop, Florida!

Acrobats at the Cirque Fernando (Francisca and Angelina Wartenberg), 1879. Pierre-Auguste Renoir. *Art Institute of Chicago.*

This undated glass negative of Bertha Palmer shows her channeling the same Orientalist spirit that animated the Ziegfeld Follies and Alfred Cheney Johnston's photography. *Chicago History Museum.*

FLORIDA

GRAPE FRUIT AND ORANGE GROVES.
BEAUTIFUL WINTER HOMES.
FRUIT AND VEGETABLE LANDS

in the famous Sarasota Bay district of Manatee County, on the gulf. I am one of the largest growers and land owners in Manatee County and can furnish you with any kind or size property desired. I also improve lands and raise groves for purchasers. Best location in U. S. Lowest prices. Easy terms. Call or write for free book and full information.

J. H. LORD, Owner. 922 Marquette Bldg.

FOR SALE—
A REAL BARGAIN IN FLORIDA LAND.

I want to get in touch with a number of clean, cut people who would be interested in a mutual benefit proposition. Have recently returned from a two weeks' trip to Manatee County, Florida, where I went to inspect this land and locality. I selected a choice piece of land and in order to get just what I desired it was necessary for me to purchase the entire tract. NOW THEN, I AM NOT IN THE LAND BUSINESS, but here is what it is. It is near the Royal Palm nurseries and adjoins the British Honduras Co., 800 acre tract now being developed—is surrounded by numerous orange and grape fruit groves and truck farms; right on the railroad; half mile from town, three and a half miles from Bradentown [county seat]. Manatee river and Sarasota bay on the gulf coast; lands of this character now being sold for $50 to $100 per acre. I will sell only 52 tracts—of ten acres or more of this land at $30 per acre. Terms to suit. Money no object. No interest or taxes to pay. If interested address N 388, Tribune.

Top: According to biography *Silhouette in Diamonds*, Bertha moved to Sarasota, Florida after seeing a *Chicago Tribune* ad. If true, the ad is probably this one from January 16, 1910.

Bottom: Only one other ad fits the *Silhouette in Diamonds* story: *Chicago Tribune* January 23, 1910. The British Honduras Co. owned adjacent land.

Bertha Palmer is credited with developing Sarasota, Florida, through her business acumen. She certainly bought land and developed it, but Chicago families were already wintering in the area.[76] Armour was building railways just to the north in St. Petersburg;[77] the Queen & Cresent railway already operated a Sarasota station by February 1910.[78] That fateful spring of 1910, Bertha followed her husband's business contacts down to the Sunshine State while Chicago's sex trade was left to "the help" like Al Capone.

CONCLUSION

Chicago has been christened the "Second City," but its organized crime element has played a first-tier role shaping the politics and culture of the United States. That influence flowered through institutions like the Board of Trade, but its roots are firmly in prairie soil. Selling the votes, labor and even the bodies of Midwesterners provided the foundation of a "Central Empire."

This empire was the product of older political factions and organized crime fleeing reversals back East. The sad spectacle of Chicago's modern Democratic Machine is nothing more than the logical conclusion of policies that privileged families like the Honorés and Sewards pursued to achieve and maintain power.

Local histories can offer a grassroots perspective on a national problems. In the history of Monroe, Wisconsin, and particularly that of Arabut Ludlow and Bone Latta, we see broad historical forces shaping personal actions. No doubt Lincoln's sponsors felt his counterfeiting taint would disappear with the records of contemporary Secret Service investigations. Instead, the efforts of generations of Midwestern historians preserved the court cases, pardon paperwork, newspaper reports and sometimes even firsthand accounts that have allowed a fuller story to be told.

The legacy of Arabut Ludlow and his peers is also felt in Wisconsin's public education.[1] Green County's administrators were from the first driven to standardize and control childhood education based on East Coast models, and this caught the attention of educators in the state capital, Madison.[2]

Monroe's Union School District was founded in 1866 by men like C.S. Foster, J.V. Richardson, Brooks Dunwiddie, A.C. Dodge, Almira Humes's brother E.T. Gardner and her son Norman Churchill—many of these men participated in the Home Guard political violence during the Civil War.[3] They sent for Professor C.W. Twining, of an East Coast Hicksite Quaker military family,[4] to implement their vision for early childhood education and, in particular, to indoctrinate teachers.[5] Professor Twining's family included the famous Twining military men, one of whom became chairman of the joint chiefs of staff in 1957.

Hicksite Quakers adopted elements of Almira Humes's religion (Unitarianism)[6] and wanted to bring Quakerism back to its mystical hermetic roots.[7] Much like Almira's Aunt Nabby, Quakers were also preoccupied with helping children but through their conception of early education. The educational system established by Almira's peers would influence Wisconsin's educational policies for generations, right down through Monroe School Superintendent Paul F. Neverman's work at the Wisconsin Interscholastic Athletic Association.[8] Under Ludlow family patronage, Monroe's public schools would become solid military recruiting grounds even when students' parents were staunchly antiwar.[9]

There are no unimportant actors in history. Monroe, Wisconsin, is a fine example. This book shows how the actions of a banker and a hoodlum in a hamlet helped shaped the destiny of a nation. How much more about our nation's past can be learned from the quiet histories of our small towns in flyover states? If nothing else, Ludlow and Latta should inspire hometown historians to take a different look at their past. Nothing could be more salubrious for mutual understanding, and the health of our nation, than a revitalization of interest in local history.

NOTES

Introduction

1. *History of Green County, Wisconsin* (Union Publishing Company, 1884), 968 [hereafter *History of Green County* (1884)]. This authoritative account was written by an appointed committee, which included Norman Churchill, Arabut Ludlow, Josiah V. Richardson, J.A. Kittleson, N. Cornelius, T.H. Eaton, Charles A. Booth, Herman L. Gloege and J.J. Tschudy.

Chapter 1

1. David R. Johnson, *Illegal Tender* (Smithsonian Institution Press, 1995), 80.
2. By the 1870s, both the Treasury's Secret Service and Allan Pinkerton's agency called their employees "operatives." See Johnson, *Illegal Tender*, 75.
3. *Janesville Daily Gazette*, July 28, 1871, 4.
4. *History of St. Joseph County, Michigan, with Illustrations Descriptive of Its Scenery, Palatial Residences, Public Buildings, Fine Blocks, and Important Manufactories, from Original Sketches by Artists of the Highest Ability* (L.H. Everts, & Co. of Philadelphia, 1877), 47.
5. At least four witnesses called in Latta's LaCrosse/Madison trials over 1871–72 were called because they operated express offices that Latta patronized in Wisconsin and Illinois, particularly Warren, Illinois, which is just over the Wisconsin/Illinois border. United States of America v. Napoleon Bonaparte Latta, John Watson, William Watson, Case File 3; General Case Files; U.S. District Court for the Western District of

Wisconsin, (LaCrosse); Records of District Courts of the United States, Record Group 21; National Archives and Records Administration–Great Lakes Region (Chicago).

6. The top three express companies were Adams Express, American Express and United States Express, in that order. They were geographically bound and interrelated through shared directors, executives and investors. See Calvert Hahn, "U.S. Express Co," address given February 1, 1998, to the U.S. Philatelic Classics Society, New York Chapter, https://web.archive.org/web/20220707044352/http://www.nystamp.org/calvet-m-hahn-u-s-express-company/.
7. Pinkerton's apprehension of counterfeiter Jules Imbert brought him to New England financiers' attention. See James Mackay, *Allan Pinkerton: The First Private Eye* (John Wiley & Sons, 1997), 78–79.
8. Mackay, *Allan Pinkerton*, 77–79.
9. John Stewart, *Pinkertons, Prostitutes and Spies: The Civil War Adventures of Secret Agents Timothy Webster and Hattie Lawton* (McFarland, 2019).
10. Johnson, *Illegal Tender*, 75.
11. *Janesville Daily Gazette*, July 28, 1871, 4.
12. *Chicago Tribune*, July 3, 1871, 4.
13. *Janesville Daily Gazette*, July 29, 1871, 4. Lonergan, the chief of the Chicago Secret Service branch, said he did not know if Latta was ever in the "government detective service."
14. That the *Chicago Tribune* was largely accurate in its reporting is confirmed by Latta's case records in the National Archives' Chicago campus, which contain a long application from Latta's lawyers that special letters seized by Lonergan from Latta be returned. These letters detailed "private business" from 1863 to 1870 and "his [Latta's] connection with the government as a detective in the secret service." Latta's lawyers claimed that these letters were necessary for his defense. See United States of America v. Napoleon Bonaparte Latta, etc. Case File 3; National Archives, Chicago.
15. *Janesville Daily Gazette*, July 27, 1871.
16. "Tom Ballard, The Only Counterfeiter Who Knew the Secret for Making Fibrous Treasury Paper," *Chicago Weekly Post and Mail*, February 18, 1875, 1. This account lists five Ballard brothers total (Tom, George, John, Bill and Ben), all trained in carriage painting, which involved skills useful for engraving. John Dye's *Government Blue Book* confirms this on page 29. The brothers' parents were British subjects.
17. John S. Dye, *The Government Blue Book: A Complete History of The Lives of all the Great Counterfeiters, Criminal Engravers and Plate Printers* (Dye's Government Counterfeit Detector, 1880), 30. Dye describes Tom Ballard's training

with the Treasury Department in a way that strongly suggests Ballard worked at the American Bank Note Company, which was the Treasury's primary printer and engraver.

18. *Monroe Sentinel*, September 6, 1871.
19. *Monroe Sentinel*, September 20, 1871.
20. *Monroe Sentinel*, October 4, 1871.
21. *Monroe Sentinel*, September 20, 1871.
22. *The Blue Book of the State of Wisconsin, 1881* (State Secretary's Office, 487–88).
23. *Janesville (WI) Daily Gazette*, July 1, 1871, 4.
24. Mackay, *Allan Pinkerton*, 70–94; Herman Kogan and Lloyd Wendt, *Lords of the Levee: The Story of Bathhouse John and Hinky Dink* (Northwestern University Press, 2005), 53–55.
25. Mackay, *Allan Pinkerton*, 93.
26. We know from Lonergan's testimony at Latta's Janesville examination on July 28 that Lonergan had last seen Latta in Chicago on March 20 or 21 of that year, shortly after the investigation into him was begun, and that Lonergan had seen Latta "several times" before that. Therefore, we can be reasonably sure that Latta's business in Chicago was extensive by 1870, when Lonergan took his position with the Secret Service.
27. *Chicago Tribune*, July 3, 1871, 4.
28. Johnson, *Illegal Tender*, 41.
29. Tom Mitchell, "Funny Money…" and "How Did the Ballard Brothers Become the Notorious and Mysterious Watson Brothers?" *Green County Historical Society Newsletter*, September 2021.
30. During the 1850s, the "green goods game" allowed unscrupulous merchants to buy counterfeit currency through the post office. Peddlers (like Arabut Ludlow), saloon operators, hoteliers (like the Lattas back in Michigan), country merchants and even factory owners were major buyers. See Johnson, *Illegal Tender*, 41–42.
31. *Monroe Sentinel*, July 19, 1871.
32. *Monroe Sentinel*, July 26, 1871, 4.
33. *Chicago Tribune*, July 3, 1871, 4.
34. N. B. Latta faced trial from November 1871 to June 1872. See United States of America v. Napoleon Boneparte Latta, etc. Case File 3; National Archives, Chicago.

Chapter 2

1. William A. Green, "Stories Based on Fact: Republican Party Born in Allegany County," Allegany Historical Society, 2004. https://www.allegany.org.
2. *History of Green County* (1884), 350.
3. Milo Quaife, *Wisconsin, Its History and People, 1634–1924*, vol. 4 (J.S. Clark Publishing Company, 1924), 362.
4. *History of Green County* (1884), 924. E.C. Hamilton, *The Story of Monroe: Its Past and Its Progress Toward the Present* (Monroe Public School Print Shop, 1976) 131.
5. Hamilton, *Story of Monroe*, 132.
6. Charles H. Taylor, *History of the Board of Trade of the City of Chicago*, vol. 1 (Robert O. Law Company, 1917), 118–19; Paul F. Neverman, contributor, *The Wisconsin Centennial Story of Disasters and Other Unfortunate Events* (Wisconsin State Centennial Committee, 1948), 5; C.H. McClure, *The History of Missouri* (A.S. Barnes Company, 1920), 109–11; Mark W. Geiger, "Missouri Banks and the Civil War: The End of a Prosouthern Entrepreneurial Elite" (master's thesis, University of Missouri-Columbia. 2000), https://www.academia.edu.
7. *History of Green County* (1884), 947.
8. S.A. Nigosian, *Islam, Its History, Teachings and Practices* (Indiana University Press, 2004), 37–38.
9. Edward Bristow, *Prostitution and Prejudice: The Jewish Fight Against White Slavery 1870-1939* (Clarendon Press

Schocken Books, 1982); Julius Kemény, *Hungara: Ungarische Mädchen auf dem Markte* (1903).

10. Fred Donner, *The Early Islamic Conquests* (Princeton University Press, 1981), 251+. Islam was a "unifying ideology" that brought disparate military forces under one empire.
11. Susan Ritchie, "*The Islamic Ottoman Influence on the Development of Religious Toleration in Reformation Transylvania,*" *Seasons Journal* 3 (2004): 59–70.
12. Particularly via the views of William Walwyn and John Lilburne. See Rachel Foxley, *The Levellers: Radical Political Thought in the English Revolution* (Manchester University Press, 2016), 123–25; "John Biddle," *Encyclopedia Britannica*, January 1, 2024, https://www.britannica.com.
13. J. Charles Godbey, "Unitarianism and Universalism," *Encyclopedia Britannica*, October 31, 2022, https://www.britannica.com. Boehme's contribution to Universalism came from the interpretation of his ideas by his followers. See M. McClymond, *The Devil's Redemption: A New History and Interpretation of Christian Universalism* (Baker Academic, 2018), 479–87,

563–68; R. Parry, *A Larger Hope? Universal Salvation from the Reformation to the Nineteenth Century* (Cascade Books, 2019), 35–62.

14. Peitists profited immensely from Hermetic "medicine," really magic potions, based on Ottoman-curated Greek texts. The Medikamenten Expedition in Halle was the international headquarters of this undertaking and the first global pharmaceutical company. See W. Kaiser, W. Piechocki and A. Völker, "Die Anfänge einer pharmazeutischen Industrie am hallenschen Beispiel der Waisenhaus-Medikamentenexpedition" in *Parmazeutische Praxis* (1975), 187–92; V. Pugliano, "Pharmacy, Testing, and the Language of Truth in Renaissance Italy," *Bulletin of the History of Medicine* 91, no. 2 (2017): 233–73.
15. John Tolan, "Muhammad, Republican Revolutionary?" *History Today*, July 25, 2019, https://www.historytoday.com; Thomas Ross, *The Alcoran of Muhammad (*1649).
16. The life of Gerrard Winstanley, a Digger turned Quaker, is informative in this respect. See A Bradstock, ed. *Winstanley and the Diggers, 1649–1999* (Routledge, 2000), 9, 19–33.
17. "Where 50-Year Residents Are Newcomers," *Milwaukee Journal*, July 29, 1928, https://www.wisconsinhistory.org; *History of Green County* (1884), 942.
18. Reverend Jehabad Codding.
19. *History of Green County* (1884), 969; Hamilton, *Story of Monroe*, 131–32. Almira Humes is sometimes referred to as "Elmira H. Robertson" or surnamed "Churchill Robertson."
20. *History of Green County* (1884), 933.
21. *History of Green County* (1884), 826.
22. "Rev. Samuel E. Miner, Monroe," entry in *The US Biographical Dictionary and Portrait Gallery of Eminent and Self-Made Men, Wisconsin Volume* (American Biographical Publishing Company, 1877), 226.
23. *History of Green County* (1884), 1,095.
24. *History of Green County* (1884), 933–34.
25. Hamilton, *Story of Monroe*, 17, 131–32. Ludlow sold goods there as a young itinerant peddler.
26. Catherine Holder Spude, "Brothels and Saloons: An Archaeology of Gender in the American West," *Historical Archaeology* 39, no. 1 (2005): 89–106.
27. Hamilton, *Story of Monroe*, 131.
28. K. Anne Ketz,Elizabeth J. Abel and Andrew J. Schmidt, "Public Image and Private Reality: An Analysis of Differentiation in a Nineteenth-Century St. Paul Bordello," *Historical Archaeology* 39, no. 1 (2005): 74–88.
29. *History of Green County* (1884), 349.

30. Monroe's *Sentinel* newspaper, "The Story of a Pioneer's Life," July 10, 1893, 4.
31. Hamilton, *Story of Monroe*, 131.
32. According to *History of Green County* (1884), this journey was subsidized by Silas Gardner's "Masonic fraternity" after his 1817 death (see page 364). Freemasonry would come under intense public criticism after the murder of William Morgan in 1826.
33. No official record of this marriage available.
34. Hamilton, *Story of Monroe*, 131.
35. Edward Bristow, *Prostitution and Prejudice: The Jewish Fight Against White Slavery 1870–1939* (Schocken Books, 1982), 142–43, 178–79. Older prostitutes found themselves in frontier locales like Monroe, Wisconsin.
36. Matt Figi, *Becoming a Village: Monroe in the 1850s* (Matt Figi, Monroe, WI, 2009); also, *Pictorial History of Monroe, WI* (Matt Figi, Monroe, WI, 2006).
37. H.F. Kett & Company, *The History of Jo Daviess County, Illinois* (Chicago, 1878), 828. For more on Galena, Illinois, see John Reynolds, *Reynolds' History of Illinois* (Chicago Historical Society, 1879), 169.
38. These Galena men were like Monroe's business elite. George R. Jones, "Joseph Russell Jones (1823–1909): A Tale of Two Cities and the Destiny of Crossing Paths with the Likes of Grant and Lincoln," Belvedere Mansion and Gardens, https://www.belvederemansionandgardens.com.
39. Many agents were criminals themselves. See Johnson, *Illegal Tender*, 75.
40. Hamilton, *Story of Monroe*, 17, 131–32; *History of Green County* (1884), 924, 931.
41. Payne shot John Bringold, who had just bought Payne's Buckhorn Tavern, in a quarrel over a railway fence. Payne fled to California, but prior to this violent episode he was active in founding Monroe as the county seat. See Bob Elmer, *Green County (WI) Historical Society Newsletter*, December 2021.
42. Hamilton, *Story of Monroe*, 131; Wisconsin Historical Society, Madison, WI, USA, Wisconsin Marriage Records Pre-1907. They were actually married on September 28, 1842.
43. Hamilton, *Story of Monroe*, 42–44. Helen Bingham, *History of Green County, Wisconsin* (Burdick & Armitage, Printers, 1877) [hereafter *History of Green County* (1877)],125.
44. Bingham, *History of Green County* (1877), 125.
45. "Banking House of Dunlevy, Delano & Co," *The Western Star* (Lebanon, OH), January 9, 1852, 4, Q4.
46. Joseph Patterson Smith, *History of the Republican Party in Ohio*, vol. 1 (Lewis Publishing Company, 1898), 713.
47. Edward Chauncey Marshall, *The Ancestry of General Grant, and Their Contemporaries* (Sheldon & Company, 1869), 169.

48. "Monroe Township Map," in *Green County Plat Map, 1861* (Green County Historical Society).
49. Hamilton, *Story of Monroe*, 44–45.
50. "Bingham Lead the Way," *The Monroe Sentinel*/First National Bank commemorative pamphlet (not newspaper). June 22, 1981. Collection of the Green County Historical Society.
51. *History of Green County* (1884), 421.
52. *History of Green County* (1884), 546.
53. *History of Green County* (1884), 945.
54. *History of Green County* (1884), 439, 927.
55. *Monroe Evening Sentinel*, September 20, 1871.
56. John S. Minard, *Allegany County and Its People, a Centennial Memorial History of Allegany County, New York, Illustrated* (W.A. Fergusson & Co., 1896), 104.
57. *History of Green County* (1884), 429.
58. D.W.C. Littlejohn was a Temperance Whig. He was also chairman of the New York State Congress Canal Committee and served with Chicago's Thomas Richmond, of Richmond House, on a committee to petition the secretary of war to improve navigation conditions on the St. Clair Flats waterway between Canada and Detroit, Michigan. See *Hornellsville Weekly Tribune*, February 15, 1855; "The Legislature," *Buffalo Courier*, January 2, 1854; "Appropriation for the Canals," *Brooklyn Daily Eagle*, March 22, 1854; "The Marine Convention," *Buffalo Courier Express*, March 13, 1854.
59. "The Know Nothings and the Know Nothing Oath," *New York Daily Herald*, February 8, 1855, 8, Q1.
60. "Highly Important from Albany," *New York Daily Herald*, February 7, 1855; "Waifs from the Albany Legislature," *New York Daily Herald*, February 8, 1855; "The Recent Election of Wm H Seward," *New York Daily Herald*, February 12, 1855.
61. *New York Tribune*, February 8, 1855.
62. *History of Green County* (1884), 537–38, 826; Hamilton, *Story of Monroe*, 40.
63. *History of Green County* (1884), 536.
64. *History of Green County* (1884), 536.
65. A full list of the "military company" can be found on page 537 of *History of Green County* (1884). Some names were slightly mispelled on 1871/72 subpoenas, but the men can be identified beyond reasonable doubt by cross-checking against the 1860 Monroe Population Schedule as printed in *Becoming a Village: Monroe, WI in the 1850s* by Matt Figi, Green County Historical Society.
66. *History of Green County* (1884), 538.
67. Bingham, *History of Green County* (1877), 129–30.

68. A full list of members of this "judicial committee" can be found on page 538 of *History of Green County* (1884).
69. *History of Green County* (1884), 539.
70. Rupp wrote much of the Civil War material available at the Green County Historical Society, 1617 Ninth Street, Monroe, Wisconsin, https://www.gcwihs.org.

Chapter 3

1. *Monroe Sentinel*, August 9, 1871.
2. *History of Green County* (1884), 930.
3. *History of Green County* (1884), 927.
4. *Monroe Sentinel*, September 20, 1871.
5. Figi, *Becoming a Village*, 56.
6. *Monroe Sentinel*, August 30, 1871, and March 6, 1872.
7. The *Monroe Sentinel* had been set up as a Republican Party mouthpiece by Lincoln partisans. See *History of Green County* (1884), 582–93, 597. Over the period of the Latta investigation, the *Sentinel* was half owned by "S.E. Gardner," probably Silas E. Gardner and therefore a likely relative of Almira Humes.
8. *Monroe Sentinel*, July 5, 1871, 2.
9. "Work of Detectives," *Monroe Sentinel*, July 5, 1871.
10. Figi, *Becoming a Village*, 1–2.
11. Figi, *Becoming a Village*. See the census list on page 157.
12. *Monroe Sentinel*, September 20, 1871.
13. "Samuel Elbert Miner (1814–1904)" entry in the Thomas Minor Society's online genealogical database: https://www.tmsociety.org.
14. For example, "Aiden Lansing Miner (1805–1883)" and his descendants. Thomas Minor Society's online genealogical database, https://www.tmsociety.org. For Joshua D. Miner's life in Steuben County, New York, see "The Coniackers" *St. Louis (MO) Globe Democrat*, June 17, 1884, 4.
15. Minard, *Allegany County and Its People*, 104.
16. "Rev Samuel E. Miner, Monroe."
17. See the "Philo Minor (1780–1832)" entry in the Thomas Minor Society's online genealogical database, https://www.tmsociety.org. Louisa's father descended from Manassah Minor's brother John Miner (1635–1719), both of Connecticut. (There was considerable spelling variation of the family surname.) Sources listed for Louisa's information are "Ohio, County Marriages, 1789–2013," database with images, FamilySearch, https://familysearch.org; Stephen Youngs and Lois Miner, October 9, 1835; citing Geauga, Ohio, United States, reference

P696 ML; county courthouses, Ohio; FHL microfilm 873,464; "Ohio Marriages, 1800–1958," database, FamilySearch https://familysearch.org , Stephen Youngs and Lois Miner, October 9, 1835; citing Cluster, Geauga, Ohio, reference; FHL microfilm 20,256.

18. We met Daniel S. Young, Stephen and Louisa's boy, earlier as a member of the "Royal Arcanum." See 1870 Census Records for Louisa Young and Danl (or Daniel) Young of Monroe, Green County Wisconsin, Ancestry.com.
19. Stephen Young and Lois/Louisa Miner were married in Geauga, see Geauga County, Ohio Marriage Records, October 20, 1835. Their first child, Daniel, was born in Stephenson County, Illinois, on August 12, 1838. Given the difficulties inherent in traveling while pregnant, it's likely the Youngs left Geauga between November 1835 and November 1837, which includes the window of failure of the Kirtland Safety Society (August/September 1837).
20. Kathleen Kimball Melonakos, *Secret Combinations: Evidence of Early Mormon Counterfeiting 1800–1847* (Lyrical Productions, 2018), 21–39.
21. "The Career of Josh Miner," *New York Times*, March 13, 1886, 5.
22. *US Biographical Dictionary* (1877), 225–28.
23. Otto Scott, *The Secret Six: John Brown and the Abolitionist Movement* (Uncommon Books, 1993).
24. William Cothren, *History of Ancient Woodbury, Connecticut*, vol. 3 (Woodbury, 1879), 176, 252.
25. "Justus Minor," Thomas Minor Society, https://tmsociety.org. Justus's children are all recorded as "Miners," so this surname spelling change happened under Justus's watch.
26. William Cothren, *A History of Ancient Woodbury*, vol. 1 (Woodbury, 1871), 243.
27. "Marinus Willett Miner," Thomas Minor Society, https://tmsociety.org. Marinus and his wife spent their life around Allegany County, New York. The *New York Times*, March 13, 1886, reported Joshua Miner as sixty–two when he died that year, making his birth year 1824, the year of Marinus Willett Miner's marriage to his wife, Amanda (Nye) Miner. The pair's first acknowledged child was Juliette, born three years later in 1827.
28. "The Coniackers," *St. Louis (MO) Globe-Democrat*, June 17, 1884, 4.
29. Absalom Miner died in Friendship, Allegany County, New York, the birthplace of the Republican Party. See "Absalom Miner (1771–1854)," Thomas Minor Society, https://tmsociety.org/.
30. Katherine Smoak, "The Weight of Necessity: Counterfeit Coins in the British Atlantic World, circa 1760–1800," *William and Mary Quarterly* 74, no. 3 (July 2017): 467–502.
31. "Coniackers."

32. See the entries for "Asher Wetmore Miner (1814–92)" and "Daniel C. Miner (1812–93)," Thomas Minor Society, https://tmsociety.org.
33. "Rutherford B. Hayes" entry in "About the White House," The White House, https://www.whitehouse.gov; "Latta Pardoned," *Wisconsin State Journal*, April 3, 1877, 1.

Chapter 4

1. *Chicago Tribune*, November 30, 1870, 4.
2. *Chicago Evening Mail*, December 28, 1870. There were a number of skilled German counterfeiters working stateside at this time, see also Dye, *Government Blue Book*. This is important in chapter 7.
3. *Chicago Evening Mail*, December 2, 1870. Page 1.
4. "More Secret Work," *Chicago Tribune*, August 7, 1871, 1.
5. Kentucky's governor at this time was Lazarus Whitehead Powell, who was President Buchanan's choice to parley with Brigham Young in the wake of the Mountain Meadows Massacre of 1857. See his entry in National Governors' Association biographical database, https://www.nga.org.
6. "Arrests of a Gang of Dealers in Counterfeit Bank Notes and Bogus Coin in Rush, Bartholomew, Decatur, and Delaware Counties," *Mineral Point (WI) Tribune*, August 25, 1857, 2, Q2. Also, see note 8 in this section.
7. Alexander T. Haimann, "Rawdon, Wright, Hatch & Edson (1847–1851)," Smithsonian National Postal Museum, https://postalmuseum.si.edu.
8. Joseph Carlos Marin, "Well Calculated and Intended to Deceive: Counterfeiting and Policing along the Ohio and Mississippi Rivers during the Mid-Nineteenth Century," (PhD diss., Florida International University, 2020).
9. *Annual Report of the Auditor for the State of Ohio* (1853), 15.; *Documents, Including Messages and Other Communications Made to the Fifty-First General Assembly of the State of Ohio*, vol. 18, part 1 (Columbus, Osgood, Blake, and Knapp Printers, 1854), 319.
10. William H. Griffiths, *The Story of the American Bank Note Company* (American Bank Note Company, 27–48, 91); Alexander T. Haimann, "Rawdon, Wright, Hatch & Edson (1847–1851)" Smithsonian National Postal Museum. https://postalmuseum.si.edu.
11. "Neziah Wright," in *American Numismatic Biographies*, Pete Smith (Self-published, 2023), 455. https://nnp.wustl.edu/library/book/623479.
12. "Neziah Wright," 455.
13. Stephen Mihm, *A Nation of Counterfeiters, Capitalists, Con Men, and the Making of the United States* (Harvard University Press, 2007), 66–67.

14. "Coniackers."
15. Ohio History Connection Archives, Governor Chase Pardon Papers, SAS (State Archives Series) 669.
16"Going Home To Vote," a pamphlet of Chase's campaign-trial speeches, as quoted by the U.S .Treasury Department, "Salmon-Chase-Photo," https://home.treasury.gov.
17. Salmon P. Chase and John Niven, ed., *The Salmon P. Chase Papers*, vol. 1, *Journals 1829–1872* (Kent State University Press, 1993) 179, 161, 167–68, 171, 186, 192, 195, 206.
18. Walter Stahr, *Salmon P. Chase, Lincoln's Vital Rival* (Simon & Schuster, 2022), 62. Emphasis added.
19. Chase and Niven, *Salmon P. Chase Papers*, 1:184–85.
20. Walter Stahr, *Seward: Lincoln's Indispensable Man* (Simon & Schuster, 2012), 66.
21. James Gigantino II, *William Livingston's American Revolution* (University of Pennsylvania Press, 2018), 4.
22. Gigantino, *William Livingston's American Revolution*, 13, 26–30.
23. The Livingstons were New York City's preeminent brothel landlords. See Edwin G. Burrows and Mike Wallace, *Gotham: A History of New York City to 1898* (Oxford University Press, 1998), 484; Timothy J. Gilfoyle, *City of Eros: New York City, Prostitution, and the Commercialization of Sex, 1790–1920* (W.W. Norton & Company, 1994), 43, and from page 317+ a shocking list of brothels owned by John R. Livingston.
24. Robert "the elder" Livingston was a business partner of the notorious pirate Captain William Kidd. See Edwin Brockholst Livingston, *The Livingstons of Livingston Manor* (Knickerbocker Press, 1910), 71–102. Later Livingstons would profit from wartime smuggling. Gilfoyle, *City of Eros*, 43.
25. Howard Zinn and Anthony Arnove, *Voices of a People's History of the United States* (Seven Stories Press, 2009), 76; Richard Hofstadter and Michael Wallace, *American Violence* (Knopf Doubleday Publishing Group, 2012), 115–18.
26. Peter Cutul, "Land Heist in the Highlands: Chief Daniel Nimham and the Wappinger Fight for Homeland," NYS Office of Parks, Recreation and Historic Preservation, https://www.hhlt.org.
27. Irving Mark and Oscar Handlin, "Land Cases in Colonial New York (1765–1767): The King v. William Prendergast," 19 *NYU Law Review* 165 (1941–1942); Irving Mark, "Agrarian Revolt in Colonial New York, 1766," *American Journal of Economics and Sociology* 111 (1942).
28. Gigantino, *William Livingston's American Revolution*, 111–19.
29. Gigantino, *William Livingston's American Revolution*, 170–71, 188–97.
30. Stahr, *Salmon P. Chase*, 89–90.

31. Glyndon Van Deusen, *Thurlow Weed: Wizard of the Lobby* (Little, Brown and Co., 1947), 225.
32. Chase and Niven, *Salmon P. Chase Papers*, 1:245; Stahr, *Seward*, 146–53.
33. Stahr, *Salmon*, 124.
34, "The Kansas-Nebraska Act, May 30 1854," *Historical Highlights*, United States Senate, https://www.senate.gov.
35. William G. Thomas, "The Growth of Slavery and Southern Railroad Development" as part of *Railroads and the Making of Modern America* (Digital History Project), University of Nebraska–Lincoln, 2006–2017, https://railroads.unl.edu/views/item/slavery.
36. Tom Calarco, *People of the Underground Railroad: A Biographical Dictionary* (Greenwood Press, 2008). Railway towns like Waterloo, Iowa, saw their Black population grow as railroads made their relentless march westward and magnates sought to break strikes, See David Jackson, Joyce Zhuojun Chen, "The Early History of Illinois Central Railroad Company in Waterloo (1860–1900)," African American Voices of the Cedar Valley, https://aa-voices-museum.uni.edu. This migration was sometimes accompanied by a rise in Republican-sponsored, pro-saloon organized crime and police corruption. See Roberta Senechal de la Roche, *In Lincoln's Shadow : The 1908 Race Riot in Springfield Illinois* (Southern Illinois University Press, 2008): 79–84; Brian Dolinar, *The Negro in Illinois* (University of Chicago Press, 2013), 59–60. These problems may have been a long time coming: evidence of 1860s-era urban organized crime recruiters piggybacking off of shady Union "labor brokers" (legalized trafficking) to recruit dislocated Blacks is offered in *Freedom: A Documentary History of Emancipation*, series 3, vol. 1, *Land and Labor*, edited by Ira Berlin, Steven Hahn, René Hayden (University of North Caroline Press, 2017), 503, 535–37.
37. Edna Bonacich, "Abolition, The Extension of Slavery and the Position of Free Blacks: Split Labor Markets in the United States 1830–63," *American Journal of Sociology* 81, no. 3 (November 1975): 601–28.
38. Stahr, *Seward*, 154.
39. Trudy Krisher, *Fanny Seward: A Life* (Syracuse University Press, 2015), 45–46.
40. Matthew Pinsker, "The Underground Railway," Online Resource for the National Humanities Center, https://americainclass.org.
41. Pinsker, "Underground Railway."
42. Noelle K. Brigden, "Underground Railroads and Coyote Conductors: Brokering Clandestine Passages, Then and Now," *Int. J. Migration and Border Studies* 5, nos. 1–2 (2019).
43. David W. Blight, *Passages to Freedom: The Underground Railroad in History and Memory* (Smithsonian Books, 2004), 98.

44. Chase and Niven, *Salmon P. Chase Papers*, 1:244.
45. Mackay, *Allan Pinkerton*, 84.
46. James D. Horan, *The Pinkertons: The Detective Dynasty that Made History* (Crown Publishers, 1967), 38.
47. Stahr, *Seward*, 154.

Chapter 5

1. *The Sun* (New York), November 4, 1871, 1.
2. *St. Louis (MO) Post Dispatch*, February 15, 1875, 2.
3. *St. Louis (MO) Globe-Democrat*, June 17, 1884; *New York Times*, March 13, 1886.
4. *The Sun* (New York), August 20, 1870; *New York Daily Herald*, July 9, 1870; "The Sleighing Carnival," *New York Daily Herald*, January 29, 1871, 8.
5. *New York Daily Herald*, October 27 1871, 10.
6. *New York Daily Herald*, March 13, 1869, 5; *The Missouri Republican*, March 13, 1869, 3.
7. *New York Daily Herald*, June 6, 1871, 10.
8. *Boston Evening Transcript*, November 23, 1871, 3.
9. *Chicago Tribune*, November 1, 1871.
10. *Reading Times*, November 6, 1871; *New York Daily Herald*, December 19, 1871, 8.
11. *New York Daily Herald*, December 15, 1871, 8.
12. *New York Daily Herald*, December 16, 1871, 11.
13. James Grant, *Money of the Mind: Borrowing and Lending in America from the Civil War to Michael Milken* (Macmillan, 1994), 43.
14. Johnson, *Illegal Tender*, 75.
15. *New York Daily Herald*, December 19, 1871, 8.
16. *New York Daily Herald*, December 19, 1871.
17. *New York Daily Herald*, December 16, 1871, 11.
18. *New York Herald*, December 13, 1871, 5; *New York Tribune*, December 13, 1871.
19. *New York Herald*, December 13, 1871.
20. *New York Herald*, December 13, 1871; *New York Daily Herald*, December 16, 1871.
21. *New York Daily Herald*, December 15, 1871, 8.
22. *New York Times*, December 12, 1871, 8.
23. *New York Daily Herald*, December 15, 1871.
24. *New York Times*, December 12, 1871, 8.
25. Dye, *Government Blue Book*, 30.
26. *St. Louis Post Dispatch*, February 15, 1875, 2.
27. *St. Louis Post Dispatch*, February 15, 1875, 2.

28. *New York Daily Herald*, December 16, 1871.
29. *New York Daily Herald*, October 27, 1871, 10.
30. *New York Daily Herald*, December 15, 1871.
31. *New York Daily Herald*, October 27, 1871.
32. *New York Daily Herald*, December 16, 1871, 11.
33. *New York Daily Herald*, December 16, 1871.
34. "Secreted Indictments: Management of the U.S. District Attorney's Office. Counterfeiters, Post Office Robbers, Smugglers, and Other Offenders Who Have Escaped Trial," *The Sun* (New York), October 10, 1872, 2.
35. *New York Daily Herald*, December 19, 1871.
36. *Chicago Tribune*, December 21, 1871, 6; *New York Daily Herald*, December 19, 1871.
37. *New York Daily Herald*, December 19, 1871.
38. *New York Daily Herald*, October 27, 1871, 10.
39. *New York Daily Herald*, October 27, 1871, 10.
40. *New York Daily Herald*, December 19, 1871, 11.
41. *Portland Daily Press*, February 16, 1872, 1.
42. *New York Herald*, December 20, 1871, 11.
43. *New York Herald*, December 28, 1871.

Chapter 6

1. Patrick D. Tyrrell sold a serialized account of the Bonelatta prosecution to multiple newspapers in 1906. For example, installments appeared in *The Menasha Record* on January 5, 1906, under the title "Stories of the Secret Service." John S. Dye's book records a P.D. Tyrrell as being an active government agent investigating counterfeiter John Peter McCartney in 1867 (page 54). Tom Ballard was actually caught with an unfinished, new-issue $1,000 Treasury note plate, according to the *New York Daily Herald.*
2. Page 10.
3. *Public Acts of the Thirty-Seventh Congress of the United States*, Sess. 1, Chap. 5, July 17, 1861, "An Act to authorize a National Loan and for other Purposes," 259–61 (This law affected fiscal year 1862); 37th Cong., 2nd Sess., Chap. 32, February 25, 1862, "An Act making additional Appropriations for the Support of the Army for the year ending the thirtieth of June, Eighteen hundred and sixty-two," a.k.a. "Legal Tender Act," 344–48; 37th Cong., 3rd Sess., Chap. 58, Section 18, February 25, 1863, "An Act to provide a national Currency, secured by a Pledge of United States Stocks, and to provide for the Circulation and Redemption

thereof," a.k.a. "National Bank Act of 1863," 665–82. A full account of the large-denomination paper bills created in the United States from 1862 onward can be found in Ira S. Friedberg and Arthur Friedberg, *Paper Money of the United States: A Complete Guide with Valuations* (Coin and Currency Institute, 2013), 50–57.

4. Zephaniah Baker, *Modern House Builder, From the Log Cabin and Cottage to the Mansion* (Higgins, Bradley and Dayton, 1857), 129–30.
5. *Dollars & Cents: Fundamental Facts about U.S. Money*, Federal Reserve Bank of Atlanta, https://www.atlantafed.org/publications.
6. Dye, *Government Blue Book*, 30.
7. Jason Dunn and David C. Wheelock, "National Banking Acts of 1863 and 1864," Federal Reserve History, July 31, 2022, https://www.federalreservehistory.org.
8. Grant, *Money of the Mind*, 48.
9. "National Bank Act of 1863," 665–82.
10. Sheridan A. Logan, *George F. Baker and His Bank 1840–1955: A Double Biography* (self-published, 1981), 18, 25.
11. George Ellis Baker, George Fisher's father, was elected to the New York State Assembly and "fastened" himself to Seward. See Grant, *Money of the Mind*, 41.
12. "Schism and Reform: Circa 1800–1900," Philadelphia Yearly Meeting of the Religious Society of Friends, https://www.pym.org. Rich Quakers owned many slaves, which challenged their "Hicksite" critics.
13. Grant, *Money of the Mind*, 49–50.
14. National Bank Act of 1863, February 25, 1863, Chapter LVIII, Section 41.
15. National Bank Act of 1863, February 25, 1863, Chapter LVIII, Section 50.
16. National Bank Act of 1863, February 25, 1863, Chapter LVIII, Section 14.
17. Grant, *Money of the Mind*, 50.
18. Grant, *Money of the Mind*, 51. Meig's comments on the FNBCNY are from his "Examiner's Report, February 23, 1872" and that of March 13, 1873.
19. Grant, *Money of the Mind*, 58–59.
20. Grant, *Money of the Mind*, 58.
21. Grant, *Money of the Mind*, 51.
22. Richard Rudolph, *Banking and Industrialization in Austria-Hungary: The Role of Banks in the Industrialization of the Czech Crownlands, 1873–1914* (Cambridge University Press, 1976); P.L. Cottrell, "London Financiers and Austria 1863–1875: The Anglo-Austrian Bank," *Business History* 11, no. 2 (July 1969).
23. "Citi Historic Records Review Summary," Citi, https://www.citigroup.com.
24. Fritz Redlich, *The Molding of American Banking: 1840–1910* (Hafner, 1951), 111.

25. Grant, *Money of the Mind*, 56. Grant in turn quotes Logan, *George F. Baker and His Bank*, 102–3.
26. Alexander Spitzmüller, *Und hat auch Ursach, es zu lieben* (W. Frick, Vienna, 1955), 90.
27. Grant, *Money of the Mind*, 59.

Chapter 7

1. For example, see Kogan and Wendt, *Lords of the Levee*; Richard C. Lindberg, *Gambler King of Clark Street: Michael C. McDonald and the Rise of Chicago's Democratic Machine* (Southern Illinois University Press, 2009).
2. The earliest reference to Ludlow's friendship with Marshall Field is in "Ludlow Theme to Fore on First National Bank's 90th Birthday," *Monroe Evening Times*, April 30, 1946: "His [Arabut Ludlow's] high top boots had the trouser legs tucked inside and he stomped along the board sidewalk.... Chicago intimates were Potter Palmer and Marshall Field, whom he visited at the old Palmer House on his trips to Chicago, boots and all." Ludlow's sons continued these Palmer House Hotel visits, and Henry, the eldest son, died there (*Wisconsin State Journal*, October 2, 1923).
3. Axel Madsen, *The Marshall Fields: The Evolution of an American Business Dynasty* (John Wiley & Sons, 2002), 33.
4. Hamilton, *Story of Monroe*, foreword, 176–69.
5. Lindberg, *Gambler King of Clark Street.*
6. "Henry Hamilton Honoré," in *The Book of Chicagoans* (A.N. Mariquis & Co., Chicago, 1911), 339; "Henry Hamilton Honoré," in *Biographical and Memorial Edition of the Historical Encyclopedia of Illinois* (Munsell Publishing Company, 1915), 774–76.
7. Carter H. Harrison IV, "A Kentucky Colony," in *Chicago Yesterdays* (Daughaday and Co., 1919), 162–78.
8. *Chicago Yesterdays*, 165.
9. *Chicago Yesterdays*, 169.
10. Donald L. Miller, *City of the Century: The Epic of Chicago and the Making of America* (Rosetta Book, 2014), 439.
11. *Chicago Tribune*, January 21, 1878, 8.
12. *Chicago Yesterdays*, 172. Turngemeinde were gymnastics clubs with liberal political overtones; many of their leaders were exiled from German-speaking lands during the revolutions of 1848 and prior reform-minded uprisings.
13. *Chicago Tribune*, November 21, 1881, 6.
14. *Chicago Tribune*, July 7, 1864, 1.

15. "The Democrats Organizing the Tramps in Indiana: Pouring in the Money to 'Set Men to Work,'" *Chicago Tribune*, August 29, 1876, 1.
16. *Chicago Tribune*, November 21, 1881, 6.
17. *Chicago Tribune*, April 7, 1885, 3.
18. *Chicago Tribune*, October 24, 1884, 10.
19. Peter Hume Brown, *The Youth of Goethe* (John Murray Publishers, 1913), 131–42, 186–87.
20. Peter H. Olden, "Anton C. Hesing: The Rise of a Chicago Boss," *Journal of the Illinois State Historical Society* 35, no. 3 (September 1942): 287.
21. The most famous of these upheavals were the 1848 Revolutions, but unrest began before then.
22. "Brentano, Lorenzo (1813–91)," Biographical Dictionary of the United States Congress, https://bioguide.congress.gov.
23. Wilhelm Stieber, *The Chancellor's Spy* (Grove Press, 1979), 2, 26–27.
24. For overview, see Paul Kengor, "The Devil in the Boxcar: How the Great War Unleashed Lenin," *Providence Magazine*, March 14, 2018, https://providencemag.com. Such operations had taken place since the French Revolution. For Johann Heinrich Merck's career see Robert J. Seidel, *Literarische Kommunikation Im Territorialstaat* (De Gruyter, 2012). Up until the United States' entry into World War I, American socialists like Mischa Appelbaum saw the Kaiser as a champion of organized labor. See "Russia Can't Win Because of Vodka," *Brooklyn Daily Eagle*, February 28, 1916.
25. Heinrich Börnstein was a theater operator in the Austrian Empire prior to his 1843–44 espionage work in France with Marx. Hapsburg theaters could not operate without police sponsorship. Börnstein oversaw the bloody occupation of Jefferson City, Missouri, on behalf of Lincoln during the U.S. Civil War. See Heinrich Börnstein, *Memoirs of a Nobody: The Missouri Years of an Austrian Radical, 1849–1866* (Missouri Historical Society Press, 1997), 3–20.
26. Börnstein, *Memoirs of a Nobody*, 8.
27. Adam-Max Tuchinsky, *Horace Greeley's New-York Tribune: Civil War-era Socialism and the Crisis of Free Labor* (Cornell University Press, 2009), ix.
28. Marx had also served Lincoln and the Hapsburgs well. Synergies between Marx's international agitation organization and Lincoln's Union army, as well as postwar Reconstruction officials, are shocking. See Robin Blackburn, *An Unfinished Revolution: Karl Marx and Abraham Lincoln* (Verso, 2011), 23–28; Walter D. Kennedy and Al Benson Jr., *Lincoln, Marx and the GOP* (Shotwell Publishing, 2023). In particular, Marx used August Zang's Hapsburg-supported *Die Presse* newspaper to stump

for Lincoln in the Austrian Empire on the eve of the Hapsburg's power loss to the Hohenzollerns. The Hapburgs used revolutionary politics to undermine their domestic opposition. See Karl Marx and Friedrich Engels, *The Civil War in the United States*, ed. Andrew Zimmerman (International Publishers, 2016,) xi–xviii; Elizabeth Adams, *A Journalist for Me: Reassessing Egon Erwin Kisch's Coverage of the Redl Affair, May 25–31, 1913.* (FeedARead.com, 2022), 119–37.

29. Stieber, *Chancellor's Spy*, 26.
30. Henry J. Tobias, *The Jewish Bund in Russia, from Its Origins to 1905* (Stanford University Press, 1972), 11–22.
31. Fred M. Schied, "Education and Working Class Culture: German Workers' Clubs in Nineteenth Century Chicago," in *Breaking New Ground: The Development of Adult and Workers' Education in North America*, 115–31, Syracuse University's Kellogg Project (1986–93) website, archived: https://web.archive.org/web/20081201233427/http://www-distance.syr.edu/schied.html.
32. Schied, "Education and Working Class Culture."
33. His-Huey Liang, *The Rise of Modern Police and the European State System from Metternich to the Second World War* (Cambridge University Press, 2002), 21–22.
34. Schied, "Education and Working Class Culture."
35. Schied, "Education and Working Class Culture."
36. Newberry Library's "Collection Overview" of its Carter H. Harrison IV's papers, https://archives.newberry.org.
37. James Green, *Death in the Haymarket: A Story of Chicago, the First Labor Movement and the Bombing That Divided Gilded Age America* (Knopf Doubleday, 2006), 119–20.
38. Stieber, *Chancellor's Spy*, 100–101.
39. Stieber, *Chancellor's Spy*, 53–59.
40. Bristow, *Prostitution and Prejudice:*, 86; Julius Kemény, *Hungara: Hungarian Mädchen auf der Markt* (Sachs & Pollák, 1903).
41. Bristow, *Prostitution and Prejudice*, 86.
42. Nancy M. Wingfield, *The World of Prostitution in Late Imperial Austria* (Oxford University Press, 45).
43. Mathieu Deflem, *Policing World Society* (Oxford University Press, 2002), 80.
44. Gilfoyle, *City of Eros*.
45. Ishbel Ross, *Silhouette in Diamonds* (Harper & Bros, 1960), 63.
46. Charles Washburn, *Come into My Parlor: A Biography of the Aristocratic Everleigh Sisters of Chicago* (Knickerbocker Press, 1934), 115.

Chapter 8

1. Lindberg, *Gambler King of Clark Street*, 28.
2. Kenneth Winn, "It All Adds Up: Reform and the Erosion of Representative Government in Missouri, 1900–2000," Missouri Secretary of State, John Ashcroft, https://www.sos.mo.gov.
3. Lindberg, *Gambler King of Clark Street*, 15.
4. Lindberg, *Gambler King of Clark Street*, 20. We met General Benjamin Butler earlier as the former employer of Secret Service head Colonel Hiram C. Whitley.
5. Lindberg, *Gambler King of Clark Street*, 19.
6. "Richmond, Thomas" entry in the "Persons" index of The Papers of Abraham Lincoln Digital Library, curated by the Abraham Lincoln Presidential Library, Springfield, IL, https://papersofabrahamlincoln.org/.
7. Benjamin P. Thomas, *Abraham Lincoln: A Biography* (SIU Press, 2008), 36–37. There is, in fact, much about Lincoln and his politics that doesn't bear scrutiny. For an introduction, see Thomas J. DiLorenzo, *The Real Lincoln: A New Look at Abraham Lincoln, His Agenda and an Unnecessary War* (Three Rivers Press, 2003).
8. *Commemorating the Underground Railroad in Canada* (Parks Canada, National Historic Sites, 2001).
9. Ed Glennan, *Surviving Andersonville: One Prisoner's Recollections of the Civil War's Most Notorious Camp* (McFarland, 2013), 6.
10. Lindberg, *Gambler King of Clark Street*, 26–27.
11. Lindberg, *Gambler King of Clark Street*, 5.
12. W.T. Stead, *If Christ Came to Chicago* (Chicago, Laird & Lee, 1894), 45–46.
13. Lindberg, *Gambler King of Clark Street*, 102.

Chapter 9

1. *Centennial History of the City of Chicago, Its Men and Institutions* (The Inter Ocean, 1905), 43–45.
2. J.W. Putnam, "An Economic History of the Illinois and Michigan Canal: I," *Journal of Political Economy* 17, no. 5 (1909): 272–95.
3. Charles Henry Taylor, *History of the Chicago Board of Trade*, vol. 1, part 1 (Robert O. Law Publishers, 1917) 116–17, 226.
4. Taylor, *History of the Chicago Board*, 117, 155, 166.
5. *Centennial History of the City of Chicago*, 45.
6. Horace Davis, *Ancestry of John Davis and Eliza Bancroft* (self-published, 1897), 25–26, 56–57.

7. Margrit Schulte Beerbühl, *The Forgotten Majority: German Merchants in London, Naturalization, and Global Trade 1660–1815* (Berghahn, 2014).
8. "Bade Farewell to Earth," *The Inter-Ocean*, March 18, 1890, 5. Scammon later became a law partner to Kentucky Colony Copperhead Buckner Stith Morris.
9. Taylor, *History of the Chicago Board*, 129–30.
10. Taylor, *History of the Chicago Board*, 125–56, 130.
11. Circumstances suggest that Queen Victoria was probably also an investor: (1) CBoT friendliness to Canadian trade routes and (2) Prince Edward's (a.k.a. Bertie) 1860 trip to Chicago, which was chaperoned by the head Galena Railway surveyor and abolitionist/Lincoln supporter Colonel Richard Price Morgan. The latter is discussed thoroughly in *History of Dwight From 1853 to 1894* by William G. Dustin, 1899. "Richard Price Morgan Dead; Was Associate of Lincoln," *Chicago Tribune*, May 21, 1910.
12. Clifford Browder, *The Money Game in Old New York: Daniel Drew and His Times* (University Press of Kentucky, 1986) 129–30, 194–95.
13. George Rogers Taylor and Irene D. Neu, *The American Railroad Network 1861–1890* (University of Illinois Press, 2003), 29, 35–36, 41–42.
14. *Evening Post*, November 25, 1837. Page 2, top LHS. Cooper Union founders Horace Greeley and William Cullen Bryant were both New York City editors, of the *NY Tribune* and *Evening Post*, respectively, who launched Lincoln's political career. Bryant was a proponent of free-trade and repealing anti-usury laws, a.k.a. "liberal" banking, which is now widely associated with globalism. In 1857, Anti-Seward "Democrats" like Rothschild banker August Belmont, John A. Dix, William Havemeyer (NYC mayor from a German "unorthodox investor" banking and sugar monopolist family) and John van Buren left the party and joined with the new Republicans, as well as "Cooper Union" reformers such as Peter Cooper, Daniel Fawcett Tiemann and Know Nothings to form a coalition that ultimately supported Lincoln. Both Seward and this disaffected Democrat camp wanted to exploit popular Know Nothing constituencies. See Edwin G. Burrows and Mike Wallace, *Gotham: A History of New York City to 1898* (Oxford University Press, 1999), 850–51, 852–68; M. Drager, "August Belmont," *Encyclopedia Britannica*, April 18, 2024, https://www.britannica.com. Lincoln appointed John A. Dix as Treasury secretary and a major general in the Union army. See "John A. Dix" entry in the Histories/Prior Secretaries section of the U.S. Treasury website, https://home.treasury.gov/.
15. Alvin F. Harlow, *The Road of the Century* (Creative Age Press, 1947), 252.

16. Carl Nyquist, "A Pioneer in the West," *Rock Island Magazine*, October 1922, 50.
17. Taylor and Neu, *American Railroad Network*, 40–41.
18. Carter Harrison IV, *Chicago Yesterdays: A Sheaf of Reminiscences*, ed. Caroline Kirkland (Daughaday, 1919), 167.
19. At about this time, Greeley described himself as a "dog about his [Thurlow Weed's] house" and a partner of "Seward, Weed & Greeley," albeit an under-remunerated one. See Stahr, *Seward*, 150.
20. Jeffery Anderson, "Joseph Medill: Legendary Tribune Publisher and Social Advocate," Medill School at Northwestern University, https://100.medill.northwestern.edu.
21. "Ray, Charles H," entry in the "Persons Index" of the Papers of Abraham Lincoln Digital Library, as maintained by the Abraham Lincoln Presidential Library, https://papersofabrahamlincoln.org.
22. Anderson, "Joseph Medill."
23. "Loan Record, A. Ludlow," book held by Green County Historical Society Archives, Monroe, WI. See "Loan Record," pages 58 and 136.
24. Charles Edward Russell, *The Greatest Trust in the World* (Ridgway-Thayer, 1905), 1.
25. Robert R. Dykstra, *The Cattle Towns* (Bison Books, 1983), 116–28.
26. Dykstra, *Cattle Towns*, 1, 126.
27. Dykstra, *Cattle Towns*, 130.
28. Ross, *Silhouette in Diamonds*, 9, 27.
29. Washburn, *Come into My Parlor*, 113.
30. Russell, *Greatest Trust*, 18.
31. Russell, *Greatest Trust*, 65–72.
32. Russell, *Greatest Trust*, 197–98.
33. *New York Times*, March 22, 1896.
34. Letter from Theodore Roosevelt to Graeme Stewart, Theodore Roosevelt Papers, Library of Congress Manuscript Division, Theodore Roosevelt Digital Library, Dickinson State University, https://www.theodorerooseveltcenter.org/.
35. Russell, *Greatest Trust*, 194–98; "The Election Case of William Lorimer of Illinois (1910; 1912)," U.S. Senate, https://www.senate.gov/. Lorimer was also instrumental reaching out to Chicago's Jews, who had largely emigrated from the Hapsburg's sphere of influence. See Dominic Pacyga, *Chicago: A Biography* (University of Chicago Press, 2009), 180.
36.Lindberg, *Gambler King of Clark Street:* 77–80.
37. Lindberg, *Gambler King of Clark Street*, 80.
38. Ross, *Silhouette in Diamonds*, 34.
39. Lindberg, *Gambler King of Clark Street*, 193.

40. Donald L. Miller, *City of the Century: The Epic of Chicago and the Making of America* (Rosetta Book, 2014), 440–41.
41. Anderson, "Joseph Medill." "In 1874, Medill purchased controlling interest in the Tribune with a $250,000 loan from friend and local entrepreneur Marshall Field."
42. Lindberg, *Gambler King of Clark Street*, 154.
43. Megan McKinney, "Inside Prairie Avenue—and Beyond," *Classic Chicago Magazine*, February 2, 2020, https://classicchicagomagazine.com.

Chapter 10

1. Howell Raines, *Silent Cavalry: How Union Soldiers from Alabama Helped Sherman Burn Atlanta—and Then Got Written Out of History* (Crown, 2023), 226.
2. Ross, *Silhouette in Diamonds*, 38.
3. Kogan and Wendt, *Lords of the Levee*, 16.
4. Ross, *Silhouette in Diamonds*, 37.
5. Washburn, *Come into My Parlor*, 27–28, 159.
6. Kogan and Wendt, *Lords of the Levee*, 19.
7. W.J. Bryan, *The Memoirs of William Jennings Bryan* (John C. Winston Co., 1925), 98.
8. Kogan and Wendt, *Lords of the Levee*, 17.
9. Kogan and Wendt, *Lords of the Levee*, 72–73.
10. Nathan Thompson, *Kings: The True Story of Chicago's Policy Kings & Numbers Racketeers* (Bronzeville Press, 2003), 32; Lindberg, *Gambler King of Clark Street*, 245. Mushmouth's gambling rackets chiefly targeted Black Chicagoans.
11. Washburn, *Come into My Parlor*, 25.
12. David Bates, *The Ordeal of the Jungle: Race and the Chicago Federation of Labor, 1903–1922* (Southern Illinois University Press, 2019), 15, 120. The Palmer House Hotel and the Post Office are identified as preferring to employ Black labor.
13. Cheyna Roth, *Between Two Wars: A True Crime Collection* (Ulysses Press, 2023), 87.
14. Abbott Kahler, *Sin in the Second City* (Random House, 2007), 92.
15. Bates. *Ordeal of the Jungle.*
16. Arna Bontemps, *One Hundred Years of Negro Freedom* (Todd, Mead & Co., 1961), 77–78; Dolinar, *Negro in Illinois*, 58.
17. David Bates, "Challenges of Race: Organizing the Chicago Stockyards, 1919," Illinois Labor History Society, May 5, 2020, http://www.illinoislaborhistory.org/.
18. Kahler, *Sin in the Second City*, 179–80; Kogan and Wendt, *Lords of the Levee*, 321.

19. "Mann White Slave Act Is Held Constitutional: Jack Johnson Loses Fight in Appeal," *Monroe Evening Times*, February 24, 1913.
20. "Low Pay Causes White Slavery," *Monroe Evening Times*, March 8, 1913; Bristow, *Prostitution and Prejudice*, 26–27.
21. Madsen, *Marshall Fields*, 12. Across the globe, madams use debt slavery to control prostitutes, and buying expensive "work clothes" on credit was a typical nineteenth-century modus operandi.
22. Kogan and Wendt, *Lords of the Levee*, 341.
23. Virgil Peterson, *Barbarians in Our Midst: A History of Chicago Crime and Politics* (Pickle Partners Publishing, 2018), 62; Kogan and Wendt, *Lords of the Levee*, 78.
24. Washburn, *Come into My Parlor*, 115.
25. Kogan and Wendt, *Lords of the Levee*, 76–78, 233; Pacyga, *Chicago*, 241.
26. Neil Gale and Brian Lloyd, "The History of Chicago's 'Red-Light' Vice Districts [PG-13]," *Digital Research Library of Illinois History Journal*, January 2017, https://drloihjournal.blogspot.com/.
27. Robert M. Lombardo, *Organized Crime in Chicago: Beyond the Mafia* (University of Illinois Press, 2012), 61.
28. Ross, *Silhouette in Diamonds*, 67–68.
29. Katherine Vecchio, "Little Egypt: A Critical Biography," *CUNY Academic Works*, https://academicworks.cuny.edu.
30. Vecchio, "Little Egypt."
31. Joel Best, "Careers in Brothel Prostitution: St. Paul, 1865–1883," *Journal of Interdisciplinary History* 12, no. 4 (Spring 1982): 597–619.
32. Keely Stauter-Halsted, *The Devil's Chain* (Cornell University Press, 2015), 152.
33. Bristow, *Prostitution and Prejudice*, 191.
34. "Chicago, 3 October 1893," entry in *Franz Ferdinand's World Tour: Archduke Franz Ferdinan's Notes from His Voyage Around the World 1893*, http://www.franzferdinandsworld.com.
35. "Presented to Mme. Sofia Scalchi: Five Hundred Chicagoans Meet the Great Singer at the Hotel Metropole," *Chicago Tribune*, December 4, 1891.
36. Florence Ziegfeld, "The Peace Jubilee 1872: Dr. Ziegfeld's Memories," *The Philharmonic* 1, no. 1 (January 1901).
37. Nancy M. Wingfield, *The World of Prostitution in Late Imperial Austria* (Oxford University Press, 2017), 199.
38. *Chicago Tribune*, October 16, 1892, 15.
39. Robert Hudovernik, *Jazz Age Beauties: The Lost Collection of Ziegfeld Photographer Alfred Cheney Johnston* (Universe, 2006).

40. For an overview, see Dag Herbjørnsrud, "The Untold Story of India's Vital Atheist Philosophy," Blog of the American Philosophical Association, June 16, 2020. https://blog.apaonline.org.
41. Ian Brooks Reed, "Rammohan Roy and the Unitarians" (master's thesis, Florida State University, 2015),
42. P. Mason, "Lord William Bentinck," *Encyclopedia Britannica*, September 10, 2023, https://www.britannica.com; Uma Dasgupta, *Science and Modern India* (Pearson India, 1900), 507n23; Robert Whitaker, "Utilitarianism" in *The British Empire: An Historical Encyclopedia*, vol. 1, ed. Mark Doyle (Bloomsbury, 2018), 72–73. This school was the Church of Scotland's "General Assembly's Institution" in Calcutta, now called the Scottish Church College, and was founded with the support of Lord William Bentinck, champion of the British East India Company. Bentinck's contentious "Westernization" projects were inspired by Jeremy Bentham and John Stuart Mill, who served a role analogous to the company's spymaster. For information on the Mill family and their role with the BEIC, see Eric Stokes, *The English Utilitarians and India* (Oxford University Press, 1959); Abram L. Harris, "John Stuart Mill: Servant of the East India Company," *Canadian Journal of Economics and Political Science* 30, no. 2 (1964): 185–202; William Foster, *The East India House* (John Lane, 1924) 193–225; C.H. Phillips, *The East India Company 1784–1834* (Manchester University, 1940): 339–40.
43. Sophia Dobson Collet, *The Life and Letters of Raja Rammohun Roy*, ed. Hem Chandra Sarkar (Calcutta, 1914), 16, 17; Rajagopal Chattopadhyaya, *Swami Vivekananda in India: A Corrective Biography* (Motilal Banarsidass, 1999) 29; Judith Margaret Brown, *Modern India: The Origins of an Asian Democracy* (Oxford University Press, 1994), 161–63; Elizabeth de Michelis, *A History of Modern Yoga: Patanjali and Western Esotericism* (Continuum, 2004): 42–50.
44. Lynn Zastoupil, "Defining Christians, Making Britons: Rammohun Roy and the Unitarians," *Victorian Studies* 44, no. 2 (2002): 215–43.
45. Sreejit Datta, "Was Raja Rammohun Roy a 'British Stooge'?" News18, June 9, 2023, https://www.news18.com.
46. John L. Brooke, *The Refiner's Fire: The Making of Mormon Cosmology, 1644–1844* (Cambridge University Press, 1994), 10,11.
47. Martin Levey, *Ahmad ibn 'Ali Ibn Wahshiyah* (American Philosophical Society, 1966), 6; Dan Attrell, "'Bitter Poison Mixed in with Sweet Words': Psychoactive Substances and Offensive Operations in the Picatrix," The Modern Hermeticist, http://www.themodernhermeticist.com, https://www.youtube.com. *Picatrix* scholarship is the exception: Ibn Wahshiyah, a source for the *Picatrix*, explores the Indian mystic Shanaq's weaponization

of venereal disease through gifting infected "young girls" or "poison maidens."

48. Cecilia Muratori, "Chapter 9 'Platonic-Hermetic' Jacob Böhme, or: Is Böhme a Platonist?" in *Platonism* (Brill, 2020); Tomas Mansikka, "Did the Pietists Become Esotericists When They Read the Works of Jacob Boehme?" *Scripta Instituti Donneriani Aboensis* 20 (January 2008): 112–23.
49. Jean McPhail/Pravrajika Gayatriprana, "Swami Vivekananda's Contribution to the New Age," in *The Cyclonic Swami: Swami Vivekanada in the West*, eds. Sukalyan Sengupta and Makarand Paranjape (Samvad, 2005), 170.
50. Eugene Rose/Father Seraphim Rose, *Orthodoxy and the Religion of the Future* (St. Herman of Alaska Brotherhood, 1975), 21–66.
51. "Swami Vivekananda and His 1893 Speech," Art Institute Chicago, https://www.artic.edu.
52. The *Picatrix* was (probably) first translated by trader Yehuda ben Moshe. On European slavery, see Michael McCormick, *Origins of the European Economy: Communication and Commerce, AD 300–900* (Cambridge University Press, 2002). Sexual exploitation motivated the European trade.
53. Dan Attrell and David Porreca, *Picatrix: A Medieval Treatise on Astral Magic* (Pennsylvania State University Press, 2019).
54. "Renew Fight for $100,000 Estate of Mrs. Mary Spiegel," *Inter Ocean*, December 20, 1913, 3.
55. "The Strange Adventures of Christopher Columbus Crabb, Inheritor of Fortunes," *The Day Book*, April 5, 1913.
56. "1900–1911 Everleigh Club," entry in Terry Gregory's Chicagology.com. "Contemporary accounts indicate that it was he [Crabb] who sold, or leased for a long term, to the Everleigh sisters the property that housed the Everleigh club. He vainly thrust himself forward as its protector at the time of the fight to close the resort."
57. Rita Shelley, "The Everleigh Sisters' Early Days in Omaha," Douglas County (Nebraska) Historical Society, January 21, 2002, https://douglascohistory.org.
58. Wendy Jean Katz, *The Trans-Mississippi and International Expositions of 1898–1899: Art, Anthropology, and Popular Culture at the Fin de Siècle* (University of Nebraska Press, 2018).
59. Kogan and Wendt, *Lords of the Levee*, 277.
60. Ivan M. Linforth, *The Arts of Orpheus* (University of California Press, 1941), 312–13; T. Apiryon, "Dionysus," Hermetic Library, https://www.hermetic.com. Everleigh prostitutes mimicked the Titans by eating the flesh of a Dionysus-alter, thought to be a very powerful god by

Hermeticists. A similar *tableau vivant* was enacted at the opening of the 2024 Paris Olympics.

61. Kahler, *Sin in the Second City*, 76.
62. Kahler, *Sin in the Second City*, 76.
63. Ross, *Silhouette in Diamonds*, 145.
64. William G. Dustin, *History of Dwight* [County, Illinois] *From 1853 to 1894* (Dustin and Wassell, 1899).
65. Hope L. Black, "Mounted on a Pedestal: Bertha Honoré Palmer," (Master's thesis, USF Tampa, 2007); Ross, *Silhouette in Diamonds*, 193–95.
66. Ross, *Silhouette in Diamonds*, 209.
67. Ross, *Silhouette in Diamonds*, 221.
68. Ross, *Silhouette in Diamonds*, 102–4.
69. Wingfield, *World of Prostitution*, 203–4.
70. "Acrobats at the Cirque Fernando," Chicago Art Institute Collection, https://www.artic.edu. See also Ross, *Silhouette in Diamonds*, 155.
71. Stauter-Halsted, *Devil's Chain*, 104.
72. Marion Wynne-Davies, "Orange-Women, Female Spectators, and Roaring Girls: Women and Theater in Early Modern England." *Medieval & Renaissance Drama in England* 22 (2009): 19–26.
73. Frank A. Cassell, *Suncoast Empire* (Pineapple Press, 2017), 18.
74. Kahler, *Sin in the Second City*, 207–20.
75. *Chicago Tribune*, January 20, 1911.
76. *Chicago Tribune*, February 6, 1910.
77. Albert Parry Abraham Josipovich Paretsky), *Full Steam Ahead!: The Story of Peter Demens, Founder of St. Petersburg, Florida* (Great Outdoors Publishing, 1987), 15.
78. *Chicago Tribune*, February 19, 1910, 20.

Conclusion

1. *History of Green County* (1884), 350, 356–57,
2. *History of Green County* (1884), 359.
3. *History of Green County* (1884), 950–51, 962.
4. *History of Green County* (1884), 991.
5. *History of Green County* (1884), 950–63; Bingham, *History of Green County* (1877), 49–50.
6. Patrick J. Nugent, "Unitarian Belief Among Early Quakers," *A Journal from the Radical Reformation* 2, no. 3 (Spring 1993).

7. John Brooke, *The Refiner's Fire: The Making of Mormon Cosmology 1644–1844* (Cambridge University Press, 1994), 25; James De Garmo, *The Hicksite Quakers and Their Doctrines* (Christian Literature Co., 1897), 98101.
8. *2024–25 Senior Hand Book*, 3, Wisconsin Interscholastic Athletic Association, wiaawi.org.
9. For Paul F. Neverman's role abusing the 1917 Espionage Act against Green County Judge John M. Becker at Henry Ludlow's behest, see Lillian Hanson, "Espionage Case Against Judge John M. Becker" (master's degree paper in Western History, advisor Dr. Milton Longhorn, UW-Platteville, n.d.); R.B. Pixley, *Wisconsin in the World War* (Wisconsin War History Company, 1919), 87, 302.

INDEX

C

D

E

F

G

M

N

O

P

Q

R

S

T

U

V

W

Y

Z

ABOUT THE AUTHOR

Andrea Nolen is a historian from Monroe, Wisconsin. Prior to her counterfeiting research, she was a China analyst at the Council on Foreign Relations in New York City and a financial intelligence analyst for a London hedge fund.